HOPE

for the

HOME
FRONT

★ BIBLE STUDY ★

BOOKS BY MARSHÉLE CARTER WADDELL
AVAILABLE FROM NEW HOPE PUBLISHERS

Hope for the Home Front:
Winning the Emotional and
Spiritual Battles of a Military Wife

HOPE
for the
HOME
FRONT

★ BIBLE STUDY ★

WINNING THE EMOTIONAL AND
SPIRITUAL BATTLES OF A MILITARY WIFE

MARSHÉLE CARTER WADDELL

new
hope
PUBLISHERS

Birmingham, Alabama

New Hope® Publishers
P. O. Box 12065
Birmingham, AL 35202-2065
www.newhopepublishers.com

Library of Congress Cataloging-in-Publication Data

Waddell, Marshéle Carter.
  Hope for the home front Bible study : winning the emotional and spiritual battles of a military wife / by Marshele Carter Waddell.
    p. cm.
  ISBN 1-59669-033-X (softcover)
  1. Christian women—Religious life. 2. Military spouses—Religious life. I. Title.
  BV4528.15.W33 2004
  248.8'435—dc22

                    2006008131

ISBN: 1-59669-033-X

N064148 • 0806 • 4.5M1

Dedication

This is for You, Jesus.
You are my Husband,
my Warrior,
my Friend,
and my King.

Contents

Acknowledgments

Thank you, Mother, for being the spark that lit in me a burning passion for God's Word. I have many priceless memories of you, but my favorites are the countless mornings I found you sitting quietly at the kitchen table reading your Bible. I'll never forget the light in your eyes when you'd look up from the pages and smile and say, "Good morning." I knew then that I wanted that same light in my eyes.

Thank you to the precious group of ladies who allowed me to learn from them as we blazed the first trail through this study at First Baptist Church of Norfolk. Thank you for your open hearts, your candidness, your laughter, and your tears. I will always treasure you, Cindy Evans, Chafon Rogers, Cecilia McGlone, Yardley Kush, Pamela Camaya, Julie Turner, Tricia Summers, Lynette Hare, Kara Reed, April Del Rosario, Marie Raper, Stefanie Gordon, Melodie Walenius, Disa Adams, and Debora Morey. Women around the world will walk a level path through this course because you braved the trail first!

Spying Out Your Future

i praise God for you! Welcome to the first week of the *Hope for the Home Front Bible Study*! I pray that you will be encouraged and refreshed by the Lord each week as we meet together and each day as you meet alone with Him.

I challenge you and encourage you to set aside time daily to do the homework. Start your homework time with a simple and sincere prayer that God, by His Holy Spirit, will be your teacher and will show you wonderful things you do not know yet. Ask Him to silence all the other voices that are swirling around in your heart and to quiet the busyness of the day that may be clamoring for your attention. Ask Him to forgive you of anything you've done that may cause "static" or poor communication and that would prevent His full blessing on you as you seek Him. We serve a Holy God, yet I am so grateful that He is forgiving and gracious. He loves you and longs for time with you.

I thank God in advance for all He is doing and will do during our weeks together. I look forward with faith, hope, and love that He will do "immeasurably more than all we ask or imagine" in your life. I am praying for you as you look for and find hope for your home and for your life in God's Word.

★ DAY 1

*h*ave you ever thought what it would be like to have your own team of spies that you could send out ahead into your future to scope out the terrain, to spy on those already living there, and to come back and give you the lowdown? The history of the Hebrew people includes such a story.

Let me set the scene for you. The Israelites had spent 400 years in Egypt as slaves. Moses had been sent to lead them out of slavery and on to freedom. The people had witnessed many evidences that God was with them. He sent the ten plagues to soften the king's heart. He split the Red Sea for them to cross over to safety. He closed that same sea to swallow Pharaoh's advancing army. He had led them faithfully by day and by night closer and closer toward the home He had sworn to their forefathers.

At the edge of the Promised Land, the Israelites chose 12 men to be scouts. They sent them over the border into enemy territory to spy out the land and to come back with lots of information.

Read Numbers 13:1 through 14:10. As you read, listen with your heart for the purpose of the spies' mission, what the spies saw and heard, and what they reported when they returned to camp.

_____

_____

_____

_____

Was this the first time the Israelites had heard about a land God wanted to give to them? _____

What does the Lord say about that land in these Scriptures?

Deuteronomy 1:6–8

_____
_____
_____
_____

Genesis 13:14–17

_____
_____
_____
_____

Genesis 35:11–13

_____
_____
_____
_____

Exodus 3:7–8

_____
_____
_____
_____

Exodus 6:2–8

_____
_____
_____
_____

Deuteronomy 1:6–8

_____

_____

_____

⭐ ## DAY 2

*t*hink for a moment about your own life. What kind of "report" or prediction did others give you at the outset of your married life?

_____

_____

_____

Did this information encourage and equip you, or did this report make you doubtful?

_____

_____

_____

Read Numbers 13:17–20. What "intel" did Moses want the spies to bring back?

_____

_____

_____

What one piece of *physical* evidence did Moses want?

_____

_____

Why do you think Moses wanted them to bring this back with them? (Hint: Where had the people been living on their way to the Promised Land?)

_____

_____

_____

Yesterday, you read the first part of the story. Today, I want you to continue on. **Review your notes from yesterday, and then read Numbers 13:26–33.**

The times of our lives can be described in terms of terrain. There are the gentle mountains, those high points where the air is clear, where we can see for miles and miles, where we feel invigorated and revitalized and focused and "on top." There are the vineyards, those productive times in our lives, places where we prosper and are fruitful and strong. There are the streams, places of refreshment, of rest and relaxation.

But the "land" we live in also has deserts, dry and thirsty places of the heart, soul, and mind that threaten to destroy us. There are rugged mountain ranges, places that seem too difficult to cross over or travel through, lined with dramatic gorges and cliffs that throw us off balance and make us dizzy and scared. There are the raging seas that promise to swallow us alive.

Imagine that you are sent ahead into the future of your own life, fast-forwarded into tomorrow, next week, next year. As a spy sneaking a peek into your own future—based on what you've seen and heard—what would be your report of what lies ahead of you?

_____

_____

_____

_____

_____

The 12 spies came back to Moses with two kinds of reports, one great and one very grim. What would the 10 spies who pooh-poohed God's plan say about the "land" that lies ahead of you?

_____

_____

_____

_____

_____

In contrast, what would Caleb and Joshua tell you?

_____

_____

_____

_____

Which report, that of the naysayers or that of Caleb and Joshua, does your original "personal land survey" most resemble? _____

_____

_____

Why? To what do you attribute this?

_____

_____

_____

I don't want you to end your time in study today with anything negative or discouraging. **So read the verse below, savor it, take it with you in your heart throughout your day, and be greatly encouraged.**

> *"For I know the plans I have for you," declares the LORD, "plans to prosper you and not to harm you, **plans to give you hope** and a future."*
>
> —Jeremiah 29:11

DAY 3

*A*ccording to all 12 spies, the land was appealing and desirable, "flowing with milk and honey," just as God had said. **What was it then about the land that frightened them?**

Find the answer in Numbers 13:28–29.

_____

_____

_____

Read Numbers 14:1–4. It's here that I want to put something into perspective for you. About *one million* men, women, and children followed Moses out of Egypt. **How many men gave the people a negative report? (Answer: 12–2 = _____ .)** Ten! Just *ten* men with negative, unbelieving words plunged a million people into weeping, wailing, complaining, and despair. Why is it that our faith is strong as a million things go right for us, but when one very small incident allows a dose of discouragement and doubt to seep in, we buckle and collapse on the couch, weeping, complaining, and despairing?

The "land" ahead of us may already have "inhabitants" living there, too. They are the giants in our "land." These are the people, circumstances, or perceptions that discourage us, that make us want to turn around and go back to where we came from. They are the situations that scare us to death, that tower over our lives and make us feel very, very small. They are the things that make us weak in the knees and give us stomach ulcers. They are the things that make us doubt God's love for us and the faithfulness of His promises to us.

Identify two "giants" (real or imagined) that you face today.

_____

_____

_____

Are there giants looming in the opportunities and responsibilities ahead of you? What discourages you as you look over the border into the "land" ahead of you?

_____

_____

_____

Read Numbers 13:30 and 14:6–9. Amid all this chaos, two of my favorite men in the Bible speak up. What was their report?

_____

_____

_____

_____

Thank God for Joshua and Caleb! Their words and their faith are so encouraging and refreshing to me! Thank God for the "Joshuas" and the "Calebs" in my life. Were it not for their example of constant faith, positive attitude, and grip on God's goodness and faithfulness, I can't imagine where or who I'd be today.

God, in His love for you, has given you a "Caleb" or a "Joshua," to encourage you, to pick you up when you've fallen, to remind you that God is able to do everything He promised to do for you. **Write that person's name here.** _____

Your homework today ends with one more assignment. **Jot a note to the person you named above, thanking that person for being such an encouragement to you. Don't procrastinate. Encouragers need encouragement, too.**

DAY 4

*t*he Israelites acted as if this were the first time they'd heard of those other folks living on their turf. Over and over, God had told them that He was giving them "a land flowing with milk and honey—*the home of the Canaanites, Hittites, Amorites, Perizzites, Hivites and Jebusites*" (see Exodus 3:8, Exodus 3:17, and Exodus 13:5). Can't you almost hear the whiney surprise in the spies' voices as they described all these "ites" to Israel? And yet, as far as God was concerned, the land already belonged to His people. He had it all figured out already. All they had to do was trust Him to keep His word. Yes—a battle, many battles, lay ahead for them. But God had given them His word on the matter.

Likewise, God has promised you an abundant, prosperous, hope-filled life, His help, and His constant presence to be with you, not to mention a life that never ends!

Read Romans 8:28. I know, you've heard that verse one too many times. I challenge you to **read to the end of Romans chapter 8. Now, I want you to look back at the "giants" you recorded on day 3. Write them in the blanks below and reread the whole promise out loud.**

> *No, in all these things we are more than conquerors through him who loved us. For I am convinced that neither death nor life, neither angels nor demons, neither the present nor the future, nor any powers, neither height nor depth, [neither _____ nor _____ ,] nor anything else in all creation, will be able to separate us from the love of God that is in Christ Jesus our Lord.*
> **—Romans 8:37–39 (with your giants included)**

Abraham got it. He traded country and kin for a collapsible tent, then fathered a new nation that now outnumbers the stars.

Noah got it. He and his family safely rode out the worst storm in history.

Moses got it. He gave up connections with the king for something of greater value.

Joshua got it. He found courage and conquered kingdoms.

Rahab got it. Perfect protection was the result.

Gideon got it. His weakness was turned to strength, and he became powerful in battle.

Daniel got it. He came out without a scratch.

Deborah, Ruth, Samson, David, Samuel, Jeremiah, John, and Paul got it, too. Bottom line? They took God at His word. They listened and obeyed what He said.

Are you walking through a dark place?
The lamp and the light you need is His Word.

Are you trying to build a strong family, a solid business, a sure future?
The plumb line you need is His Word.

Do today's economy and markets discourage or frighten you?
The guaranteed investment you seek is His Word.

Do your prayers seem weak and empty?
The key to answered prayer is in His Word.

Do you want greater faith to face what life holds for you?
Faith is built by hearing the Word of Christ.

Do you find the world's bread stale and tasteless?
Come feast on the words that come from God's mouth.

Are you looking for permanence in an ever-changing world?
Jesus said, "Heaven and earth will pass away, but my words will never pass away" (Mark 13:31).

Do you get it yet? God gave them His word on the matter. Caleb and Joshua took God at His word. Will you?

Read John 16:33. Write a simple prayer of thanks to the One who has overcome the world and dwells with you.

_____

_____

_____

_____

Will you say yes to all that God has planned for you, or will you shrink in fear of the "giants" in the land and miss the "land flowing with milk and honey" that God has promised you?

If your answer is yes to all that God has planned for you, then lace up your hiking boots, grab your walking stick, and cinch your backpack tight. Let's explore together the land God has given us. Let's agree now to claim all of the goodness and provision God has promised us for living a life of victory over the giants of fear, anger, depression, loneliness, weariness, temptation, and self-pity.

Happy hiking!

 DAY 5

On day 5 of this first week, take a hike! Go outside. Spend time alone with God, praising Him for His provision, promises, and plans for you. Take the time to tune in to His voice as you prepare to face with faith any fears regarding your future.

Facing Fear with Faith

Welcome to our second week together! I am praying for you and believing that God is working in your heart and in your life as you seek Him and study His Word. I trust that the work you did at home last week has poured a solid foundation on which God can build your faith and your hope in the weeks to come.

DAY 1

Today you begin your own spy mission of the land ahead of *you*. Are those hiking boots working out alright? Here's an extra water bottle for your trek. Wait, what's that? Do you hear that? Is it a thunderstorm off in the distance? No, it's the sound of footsteps made by large, heavy feet! And they're coming your way! The ground under you trembles and quakes with each boom, sending shivers up your spine!

The morning fog is barely thinned by the rising sun. You can just make out the creature's looming silhouette. It continues to plod toward you, crushing everything beneath its feet with each thundering step! Birds flutter away, squirrels and rabbits scurry to their burrows. The earth settles, holds its breath, and is still as the giant stops. His towering height dwarfs and shadows you. He glares down his ugly, bulbous nose at tiny you. His yellowed, bloodshot eyes squint and focus. His chapped lips grin and thin into a sneer as he introduces himself to you.

"My name is Fear. Don't bother telling me yours 'cause your name doesn't matter to me. I find *everyone* sooner or later. Might as well turn tail and run now 'cause I'm not budging. I plan to shove my way into every corner of your mind. Don't worry. It's a *slow*, *painless paralysis* that sets in. Then I'll just stuff you inside my pouch and take you home. You'll be a delicious midnight snack."

Yikes! Let's get out of here! Wait. I hear another voice! It's also calling to you. Do you recognize it yet? It's the LORD! Can you make out what He's saying? **Turn to the Old Testament Book of Joshua and read chapter 1 to find out.**

Write what the LORD God told Joshua in verse 9.

_____

_____

_____

I like Joshua. In fact, my husband Mark and I like Joshua so much that we named our firstborn after him. We loved its meaning. *Joshua* is a Hebrew name which means "the Lord saves" or "the Lord is salvation."

Remember Hoshea, son of Nun, from Numbers 13? He was a leader of the tribe of Ephraim. Moses gave Hoshea the name Joshua (Numbers 13:16). **Based on what you learned last week about the Promised Land and its inhabitants, why do you think Moses selected the name "Joshua" from all other names he could have chosen for this particular man?**

_____

_____

_____

_____

Joshua and Caleb were two of the 12 spies Moses sent to scout the Promised Land. Joshua and Caleb were the only two spies who agreed with God about conquering the land He was giving to them.

What was God's answer to the ten *faithless* spies and the hundreds of thousands of Israelites who also chose not to believe His promise?

Read Numbers 14:20–35 and note what God said concerning:

The unbelieving generation

_____

_____

_____

_____

Their children

_____

_____

_____

_____

Joshua and Caleb

_____

_____

_____

_____

Saying no to God is always costly. Your answers to the question above spell out the price the Israelites paid in exchange for believing Fear instead of God.

They say that hindsight is 20/20. Think of a time when you said yes to Fear and no to God. **What opportunities or blessings did that decision cost you?**

_____

_____

_____

_____

The theme of the Book of Joshua is "victory through faith." The first chapter of the book is God's call for courage. The call to courage is really a call to faith. **Look back at Joshua 1:9. Was God's call for courage a *suggestion* or a *command*?**

_____

God promised to be with Joshua no matter what came his way. He assured him that "No one will be able to stand up against you all the days of your life. As I was with Moses, so I will be with you; I will never leave you nor forsake you" (Joshua 1:5). God said that he would be successful wherever he went; however, there were a few prerequisites for Joshua to experience all this.

What were the prerequisites that would guarantee God's presence and Joshua's victory?

Joshua 1:6

_____

_____

_____

Joshua 1:7

_____

_____

_____

Joshua 1:8

_____

_____

_____

Outwardly, we can put on a pretty good show for others for a while. Outwardly, we can look all put together, but inwardly, we all struggle with fear of one flavor or another—every single one of us. It seems that when we conquer one fear, another one comes along.

I'll be transparent with you. One struggle I have is the fear of flying. It's called aviophobia. It's usually irrational and always embarrassing. How about you?

What fears do you struggle with most often?

_____

_____

_____

_____

_____

I believe that God's promise to Joshua to give him victory over his fears, to never leave him, and to have success wherever he went is a promise intended for us, too. Look back at the prerequisites for having victory. **Can you complete God's formula for success?**

Courage + _____ = Success

Lots of folks have great claims to having been courageous. Few can claim success Joshua-style. **What, based on Joshua 1:6–8, was the missing ingredient in their lives?**

_____

What is courage without obedience to God? A disaster. Just ask those Israelites. I encourage you to ask God to show you if you are being fully obedient to His Holy Spirit's leading where your fear is concerned. Ask Him for the courage you need as well as the wisdom and the strength to obey Him as you face your fears today.

> *Do not let your hearts be troubled. Trust in God; trust also in me.*
>
> —John 14:1 (Jesus speaking)

DAY 2

*O*kay, for those of you who want a more in-depth study, hang on to your wigs! Read Joshua 1:9: "Have I not commanded you? **Be strong** and **courageous**. Do not be **terrified**; do not be **discouraged**, for the LORD your God will be with you wherever you **go**."

I have made five parts of this verse bold on purpose. I have done the research for you. I want you to look closely at what the deeper meanings for these words are in the original Hebrew lexicon.

Be strong: *châzaq*. To fasten upon, to seize, to be established, to hold fast, to be obstinate (!), to cure, help, repair, to fortify.

Courageous (NIV), of good courage (KJV): *'âmats*. To be alert, to be physically on foot, to establish, to fortify.

Terrified (NIV), afraid (KJV): *'ârats*. To awe, to be in awe of, to dread, to shake terribly, to be terrified.

Discouraged (NIV), dismayed (KJV): *châthath*. To prostrate, to break down by confusion or fear.

Go: *hâlak*. To walk, to go forward, to lead, to march, to be at the point (the point man!)

There are many rabbit trails that we could wander down in this one verse. I just want to point something out to you that stared me in the face as I prepared this lesson for you. Look at the definitions to the words *terrified* and *discouraged*. The first synonym for terrified and the first synonym for discouraged are things we do in the act of worship. **What are they?**

Terrified: _____

Discouraged: _____

Of course, God would not want us to be *terrified* and *discouraged* as we worship Him. Yet because the English language is not as layered as Hebrew, we miss a very important point—a *critical* point—in our study on facing fear with faith if we limit our study to just English.

Stay with me. If *terrified* and *discouraged* are similar to being in awe and to prostrating ourselves, then whom or what are we worshipping? Bowing or being in awe of or prostrating ourselves to anything else but God can be only one thing.

Read Exodus 20:4–5 and write what that one thing is.

_____

How do you think one's fear can become a form of idolatry?

_____

_____

_____

_____

_____

Father, I pray for Your forgiveness for ever bowing down or being in awe of anything but You. Thank You for opening my eyes and allowing my heart to understand this true insight about my fears for the first time. Lord, I repent of ever bowing down to my fears. You are the only One worthy of my worship, my reverence, my awe. I ask You to cleanse me from all forms of idolatry. Lord, thank You for Your patience with me and for Your readiness to forgive me again. Lord, I ask for courage and the strength I need to be obedient by saving my worship for only You. In Jesus's name, Amen.

 # DAY 3

_W_elcome to the middle of your week of study. I trust that God is tilling the ground of your heart and that you are sowing the seed of His Word there in the good soil. On day 1 of this week's study, we heard Joshua's voice tell us what God had told him as he was about to face his worst nightmare over the border in Canaan. He called to us through the Scriptures, explaining that in order to be strong and courageous we must meditate on God's Word day and night, then obey what the Lord has said to do. He passed along to us here in the 21st century God's formula for success "wherever we go": courage plus obedience equals success.

On day 2, you and I explored a word study on Joshua 1:9. We learned that in the Hebrew language *to fear, to be afraid, to be dismayed, to be discouraged* are all synonyms for elements of "worship." They included to be *in awe of* and *to prostrate oneself.* We learned that one of the key elements to overcoming our fears is to worship God alone and not to revere or fear anyone or anything else but Him.

Obedience to what God has commanded us to do and worshipping, fearing, revering Him alone are two of three discoveries I want you to make as we learn to face our fears with faith. Today you will explore God's promise of safety and deliverance and what it means to wait on the Lord. Let's get started! I'm praying for you!

Chapter 11 of Hebrews is sometimes referred to as the Hall of Faith. Read Hebrews 11. Please don't rush through this and the following exercise. By reading and answering the questions below for each person mentioned in the chapter, you will begin to see that these weren't superheroes. They were everyday folks who looked fear in the eyes, obeyed what God had commanded them, and worshipped God alone. The rest is history. The fears they faced thousands of years ago are not much different from the ones we face today.

Look at the verses in Hebrews 11 about each of the following persons and identify what may have made each person afraid. Write those fears in the space provided.

Abel—Hebrews 11:4

_____

_____

_____

Enoch—Hebrews 11:5

_____

_____

_____

Noah—Hebrews 11:7

_____

_____

_____

Abraham—Hebrews 11:8–11, 17–19

_____

_____

_____

_____

_____

Isaac and Jacob—Hebrews 11:20–21

_____

_____

_____

Joseph—Hebrews 11:22

_____

_____

_____

Moses' parents—Hebrews 11:23

_____

_____

_____

Moses—Hebrews 11:24–28

_____

_____

_____

_____

Israelites—Hebrews 11:29–30

_____

_____

_____

_____

Rahab—Hebrews 11:31

_____

_____

_____

Gideon, Barak, Samson, Jephthah, David, Samuel, and the prophets—Hebrews 11:32–38

_____

_____

_____

_____

_____

_____

How might history have been different if just one of these had chosen not to walk by faith, but rather bowed the knee and the will to his or her own fears?

_____

_____

_____

_____

We live in a connected universe. What each of us does affects another or many others. If the faithful ones listed in Hebrews 11 had been fearful ones, a domino effect would have ensued. Not only would our history books be different, but the composition and content of our Bible and the course of an entire nation would be different!

Look back over your answers. Can you relate to any of these folks? Circle or highlight all the fears above with which you identify today.

How might your life, your future, and the lives and futures of countless others be affected...

...if you stay crouched in fear regarding that which God has called you to be and to do?

_____

_____

_____

...if you step out in faith, boldly and courageously obeying God in the midst of fear?

_____

_____

_____

_____

Therefore, since we are surrounded by such a great cloud of witnesses, let us throw off everything that hinders and the sin that so easily entangles, and let us run with perseverance the race marked out for us. Let us fix our eyes on Jesus, the author and perfecter of our faith, who for the joy set before him endured the cross, scorning its shame, and sat down at the right hand of the throne of God. Consider him who endured such opposition from sinful men, so that you will not grow weary and lose heart.

—Hebrews 12:1–3

DAY 4

*i*n the fall of 1998, my husband was recalled during our long-awaited family summer vacation to be deployed to war-torn Bosnia-Herzegovina for a few months. He had returned from a six-month deployment just four weeks before. Needless to say, I was very sad, deeply hurt, and later enraged. As he hastily repacked, I reluctantly worked through the onslaught of emotions. Disappointed and discouraged, we said our good-byes.

I didn't rest well that first night. I was awakened the next morning to the news blaring from my clock radio. The reporter's announcement sent chills down my spine and a flight of butterflies through my guts. Two hours after leaving JFK, Swiss Air Flight 111 had plunged into the cold Atlantic Ocean near Nova Scotia. There were no survivors.

Mark had said that he would be flying Delta, I reassured myself, but the uneasiness remained. I moved forward through my day, hoping to hear from my husband. Finally the phone rang. My husband's voice, though crackled by the distance, soothed my fearful heart and brought tears to my eyes. He was safe at his destination, but he had a story to tell me.

Delta had overbooked his flight. Thirty-three passengers, including my husband, had been reticketed for a later flight, Swiss Air 111. Concerned about making his connections in Zurich, my husband hesitantly agreed to the changes. He sat with this rerouted group for a while. Mark, along with young couples, families with children, retired people, and businessmen, settled into their new gate lounge area.

He was uneasy about the changes. He returned to the original ticket counter, explaining that he was on military orders and simply had to make his connections in Zurich. The agent went aboard the Delta flight and announced to its passengers Mark's situation. Would anyone be willing to give up his seat for this service member, she asked. A businessman, probably in his 50s, gladly gave Mark his seat. As he exited the plane, passing my husband, Mark thanked him.

Mark's voice cracked again, this time not because of the yawning miles that separated us. No, Mark was choking back tears… tears of amazement of how, again, God had protected his life and delivered him from harm. We kept the white luggage tag with the words "Swiss Air 111" on it. The feelings we have when we look at it are almost too difficult to express.

I think about that kind businessman now and then. I thank God for him. I thank God for protecting my husband that night.

Read Psalm 27. It's a great prescription for fear. Write Psalm 27:1 here.

_____

_____

_____

_____

_____

Circle the word *salvation* above. That word in Hebrew is *yesha*. Does that sound a little familiar to you? It should. It is related to the name Joshua or *Yeshua*. *Yesha* is translated as safety, liberty, and deliverance.

Do you know that Jesus's name is the Greek form of *Joshua*? His mom, dad, brothers, sisters, and friends called Him *Yeshua*. Look back to the study for day 1 of this week. **What is the meaning of Jesus's name in Hebrew?**

_____

_____

Read Matthew 1:21. Why was *Yeshua* the chosen name for God's Son?

_____

_____

The word *save* is *sozo*, a Greek word that means "to deliver, to make whole, to preserve safe from danger."

Read Acts 4:12. The word *salvation* is *soter* in Greek. It literally means a savior, a deliverer. Where are wholeness, safety, and salvation found?

_____

Is it found anywhere else?

_____

_____

In my book *Hope for the Home Front*, I tell another story. It's about my wonderful father who, despite our years of praying for his healing, died with amyotrophic lateral sclerosis (ALS), or Lou Gehrig's disease, at 53 years young. Although it ends differently from my husband's Swiss Air 111 experience, this story is also a story of God's deliverance. You see, as I grieved for my dad, God gently taught me that true safety and deliverance is unseen to the human eye. If I believed my eyes, I would be tempted to believe that God had not protected, healed, delivered my dad in the least. I now know otherwise. In 2 Corinthians 4:18, we are told to "fix our eyes not on what is seen, but on what is unseen. For what is seen is temporary, but **what is unseen is eternal.**" By faith in what God has said in His Word about our one hope and one salvation, Jesus Christ, I know in my heart that my father experienced God's best deliverance ever…unseen and eternal…right into the presence of God.

Read Psalm 139:1–12. Is there any situation that God is unaware of in your life?

_____

Does anything happen to you that God has not designed?

_____

Is there anywhere that God cannot find you?

_____

Lou Gehrig's disease is a very dark, scary place to be. Breast cancer, divorce, financial problems, and war are, too. Read verses 11–12 again. Write your thoughts here.

_____
_____
_____
_____
_____
_____

Do not be anxious about anything, but in everything, by prayer and petition, with thanksgiving, present your requests to God. And the peace of God, which transcends all understanding, will guard your hearts and your minds in Christ Jesus.

—Philippians 4:6–7

DAY 5

*t*he Holy Scriptures tell us that there is only one legitimate fear for followers of Christ. Only one! **What is that one?**

Deuteronomy 6:13; 10:12; 31:12

_____
_____

Luke 12:4–5

_____
_____

When God commands, He rewards obedience. What are the rewards of fearing the Lord?

Proverbs 10:27

_____

_____

Proverbs 14:27

_____

_____

Proverbs 15:33

_____

_____

Proverbs 16:6

_____

_____

Proverbs 19:23

_____

_____

Proverbs 31:30

_____

_____

My daughter once asked me, how do we love Him when we're supposed to be afraid of Him? Good question. Interesting answer. Unbelievers, those who live in rebellion against God and His Son, should be afraid of God in every sense of the word. As Christians, as those who have been purchased by the blood of Christ, our sins paid in full, we fear God in the sense that we revere Him and worship Him above all others. The idea is that He is God and we are not…that He is the Creator and we are the clay…that He is the loving Father and we are the child in need of loving discipline. Big difference, don't you agree?

These verses add depth to our definition of the fear of the Lord. Write the definitions you find in each of these verses.

Proverbs 8:13

_____

_____

Proverbs 9:10

_____

_____

Psalm 111:10

_____

_____

Read Isaiah 6:1–8. Isaiah saw the Lord and cried out, "Woe is me!" He was completely aware of his unworthiness to be in the Lord's presence. **At what point did Isaiah gain the courage he needed to speak with God and to obey and serve God confidently (vv. 6–7)?**

_____

_____

_____

_____

How can we have confidence in the presence of the one and only awesome God, whom we are commanded to fear? Read Hebrews 10:19–23.

_____

_____

_____

_____

_____

Praise God for the blood of Jesus Christ! Our hearts have been cleansed from a guilty conscience and we can draw near to God with a sincere heart in full assurance of faith!

Our circumstances are designed by God. While His purposes in so designing them are many and may vary from person to person as He makes us like His Son, God's ultimate aim is to keep our will on the altar and to teach us to finally trust Him. This is the faith that pleases God.

Mark Twain once said, "Courage [we can say faith] isn't the absence of fear, but the mastery of it." How do we "master" fear?

God has given us a three-step cure for fear. It's found right here in our homework:

STEP 1:   **Obey God. Courage plus obedience to God guarantees victory.**

STEP 2:   **Pray and believe His promises.**

STEP 3:   **Fear and worship ONLY God, nothing and no one else.**

Anger and the Alternative

*a*s the wife of a US Navy SEAL, interruptions are all too common to me. There have been many midnight recalls that snatched my husband right out of our warm bed and sent him into hot spots worldwide to put out the fires caused by someone else's failed politics. These calls don't ever conveniently come during life's "commercial breaks," but inevitably during the best and favorite parts of our times together.

The ability to view interruptions and inconveniences as opportunities and the flexibility to accept them graciously are skills I am honing, but I am far from mastering. I am a planner. I enjoy brainstorming and designing fun and enrichment for my family, making the necessary arrangements, and seeing it all come to fruition. My husband and children say I am "Rabbit" of Christopher Robin's Hundred Acre Wood gang. Planners, however, like Rabbit, suffer from a chronic case of inflexibility. If it's "not on the schedule," then watch out!

Early in my marriage, when faced with an interruption, large or small, my first inclination was to impatiently demand answers from Mark as to who, what, where, when, how, and why this change of plans could possibly have taken place. *Didn't everyone know that we already had plans?* As I exhausted him of any further explanation, I could smell the smoke from the sparks of anger that were kindling a white-hot explosion deep down inside of me. Usually

I could contain the fire, but it always managed to seep out as glowing embers of searing sarcasm and unkind statements toward my beloved, inflicting wounds he did not deserve. When the frenzy passed and I was able to stew awhile, I threw a pity party for myself and mentally rehearsed for days every possible negative retort filed away in my mind.

Interruptions happen to all of us every single day. They can be as common as unwanted phone calls, disturbing doorbells, or a child's repetitive questions. They can be catastrophic, like September 11, 2001, or the unexpected death of a loved one. And somewhere between common and catastrophic are a spouse's unscheduled deployments and business trips, or an illness (someone else's or our own) that requires a total daily planner makeover. Whatever form they take, interruptions inevitably conjure up disappointment, hurt, and resentment, which all dead-end in a cul-de-sac called anger.

We've all been there at that dead end, refusing to loosen our white-knuckled grip on the steering wheel of life, gritting our teeth in rage, and trying to see through the hot tears that flood our eyes. Some of us have turned down that road so many times that we don't know the way home anymore. We just live in a state of anger, consciously or not, driving in circles, around and around again.

DAY 1

*t*his week we will take a long, hard look at anger: its definitions, types, motives, causes, and cure. Professionals who specialize in identifying counterfeit money don't spend all their time studying the fakes. They spend most of their time and effort studying the real thing. They become so familiar with the real thing—its colors, its texture, its scent, its watermarks, and its symbols—that they can spot an imitation a mile away. This principle applies to us. As we seek to live the life God intends for us, we must spend time getting to know the Real One, the Word who became flesh and lived among us. We must examine Him, His ways, His words, His fragrance, His life, in order to know and have an authentic walk of Christlike faith, not counterfeit.

In Ephesians 4:26, the apostle Paul tells us, "In your anger do not sin." That's the NIV version. The King James Bible says it this way: "Be ye angry, and sin not." It is a quote from the Old Testament, Psalm 4:4: "In your anger do not sin; when you are on your beds, search your hearts and be silent."

What do you think Paul means when he tells us, led by the Holy Spirit, to "be angry and sin not"?

_____

_____

On more than one occasion, Jesus was angry, according to the Bible. Let's look at the life of Jesus Christ for the answer to the question above. **Read Mark 11:15–17 and then John 2:13–16.**

What time of year was it?

_____

Why was there a petting zoo at the temple anyway?

_____

_____

The cattle, the sheep, and the doves were ritual-approved animals, which Jews, many of whom had traveled from very distant places, could purchase for sacrifice as required by the Lord. As for the reason for the money changers being there, the euro was not in place yet, so these traveling Jews had to convert their currencies into local cash to pay the mandatory temple tax.

How did a person who loved God feel about the temple courts?

Psalm 84:10

_____

_____

_____

Psalm 100:4

_____

_____

_____

Could anyone reverently worship God with all the mooing, bleating, and cooing going on? _____

Where did Jesus find this marketplace?

_____

_____

Jewish men weren't the only worshippers at the temple. While some would have probably liked to think they were, Jewish men weren't the only children of God. Jews and believing Gentiles, both men and women, traveled great distances, at God's invitation, to pray and to offer their gifts to Him.

Read Exodus 12:48. Who could celebrate the Passover?

_____

_____

There were, however, designated places of worship for these groups. The outer court surrounding the actual temple of Jesus's time was as close as any Jewish woman or non-Jewish person could come to God's house. It was only there that foreigners, women, and the sick could come to worship God and to pray. (Though based on ideas in Exodus 12:48, these separations were man-made. Neither in the construction of the tabernacle nor of the temple do I find one place in Scripture where God drew a line and told a certain people group, gender, or race that they were excluded from worship.)

Read John 2:15–16 again. What did Jesus _do_ first?

_____

_____

_____

Jesus did not leave us without an explanation for this display of anger. What did He teach? Read Mark 11:17 again.

_____

_____

_____

_____

Turn to Isaiah 56. Read verses 3 and 6–8. Besides Jews, whom has God invited into His presence?

_____

_____

Has God excluded anyone who "binds himself to the LORD"?

_____

Read Jeremiah 7:1–15. According to verse 6, what were the Jews *not* to do to foreigners?

_____

How did the Lord describe His house in this verse (v. 11)?

_____

God said this to the prophet Jeremiah around 600 B.C. By the time Jesus arrived at the temple that day, about how many years had God been patient with this violation?

_____

What did God promise He would do to those who had made His house of worship a "den of robbers" (v. 15)?

_____

_____

As a Jewish man Himself, Jesus's worship and prayers were not restricted in any way; He could worship inside the temple. Why, then, would He become angry?

_____

_____

_____

Another example of Jesus becoming angry is found in Mark 3:1–6. What made Him angry in this instance?

_____

_____

Jesus knew the motives behind the Jews' masquerade of compassion. They intended to bait Jesus on the Sabbath and find cause to execute Him once and for all. They had exploited the suffering of one made in the image of God, letting their traditions take precedence over compassion.

Read Philippians 2:4–5. Based on Jesus's example above and these verses in Philippians, describe one form of sinless anger.

_____

_____

What kind of attitude must govern our anger?

_____

_____

Not only was Jesus defending the rights of the foreigners, the women, and the sick of _His_ generation when He cleared the temple courts; He was, in His anger, rightly defending much more. When He twisted those cords into a whip, He was jealously defending _your rights_! Amid all the stampeding hooves of the animals and hysteric hollering of the dishonest merchants, Jesus was protecting _your_ access to the living God and _your_ place in His presence! Jesus was not thinking of Himself. He was guarding the honor of His Father's name and house as well as the treasure of His relationship with you.

DAY 2

ccording to the psalmist's instruction, "In your anger do not sin" (Psalm 4:4), we see that anger can be right and sinless.

Not all anger is wrong. The very fact that Jesus expressed anger underscores this. **According to what we covered in day 1 of this week's study, what incited Christ's anger?**

_____

_____

_____

_____

If these evoked anger from the Son of God, then it must be permissible for us to be angry when we encounter the same violations, right?_____

Yesterday, you had the opportunity to focus on a snapshot of Jesus's anger. Remember, He experienced every emotion we experience, only He *always* expressed those emotions without sinning. Hebrews 4:15 tells us that "we do not have a high priest who is unable to sympathize with our weaknesses, but we have one who has been *tempted in every way, just as we are—yet was without sin.*"

Jesus Christ is God incarnate, God made flesh, according to the Bible (John 1:14). That means that in everything He said and in everything He did, He expressed God's heart, God's ways, God's purposes, and God's personality.

Colossians 2:9 says it this way, "For in Christ all the fullness of the Deity lives in bodily form." If we fail to include God's emotions and expressions of anger, we would not be having a complete discussion on "the fullness of the Deity." We do not know God in His fullness if we pick and choose what traits we think He should have and not have. Some believers don't set foot in the Old Testament simply because they "don't like that side of God." I couldn't disagree more with that logic. If we do not embrace, study, meditate on, and submit to the *fullness* of God, our walk of faith will take on a limp due to an unbalanced view of God; therefore, today we will spend our time together taking a closer look at the Almighty's anger.

The books of the Old Testament are very clear about God's temper. The Bible's first mention of God becoming angry is with Moses during their conversation at the burning bush.

Read Exodus 4:10–14. Why do you think God was angry with Moses?

_____

_____

_____

My New Year's resolution in 2000 was to read the Bible from cover to cover. In the first month or so, I breezed along, enjoying the accounts of the creation and stories of Abraham, Isaac, and Jacob and sons. Wide-eyed and munching on every word as if it were movie popcorn, I eagerly consumed the exciting scenes of God freeing the Israelites from Egypt, and splitting the sea so their sandals would stay dry as they left the land of their slavery forever. Sometime around March of that year, my journey through the Scriptures became more difficult as I encountered books like Leviticus, and later, Isaiah, Jeremiah, and Ezekiel. I was no longer at a comfortable cruising altitude. I was encountering turbulence with a capital T! I hung on for dear life as, chapter after chapter, the writers described in detail the terrible anger of Almighty God. Day after day, I leaned into the winds of His wrath and trudged forward, determined to reach my goal by year's end. There were many days I had to come up for air and read a verse or two from the New Testament, gasping for grace!

"O LORD, do not rebuke me in your anger or discipline me in your wrath" (Psalm 38:1). David prayed that God would not treat him as he deserved to be treated. He asked God not to discipline him in His wrath. **Why would he ask this? What did David know about God's anger and wrath that would stir up such a request? Let's find answers to these questions by going to God's Word.**

Read Psalm 78. How had God displayed His anger in the past?

_____

_____

_____

_____

_____

_____

_____

Read the following verses and write what provoked God to anger in the past.

Numbers 11:1

_____

_____

Numbers 11:4–10

_____

_____

_____

Numbers 12:1, 5–9

_____

_____

_____

Numbers 14:11–12, 22–23

_____

_____

Exodus 32:7–10 (pay particular attention to v. 9)

_____

_____

_____

Deuteronomy 4:25

_____

_____

Deuteronomy 6:13–16

_____

_____

_____

Digging deeper: For those of you who don't have a baby crying, something boiling over on the stove, or a doorbell ringing, read Deuteronomy 32, especially verses 5–6 and 15–43, for a summary of why God was angry with unbelieving Israel.

> _For the LORD your God is a consuming fire, a jealous God._
> —Deuteronomy 4:24

When the Bible speaks of God's anger, many times the writer says something or someone "kindled" the Lord's anger. **When you think of the word "kindling," what comes to mind?**

_____

_____

Read Exodus 34:4–7. How does God describe His own anger? _____

This description of God's anger was a comforting truth that the people of God held onto throughout the centuries (and still do!). Prophets and writers reminded them time and again (Numbers 14:18, Nehemiah 9:17, Jonah 4:2, Nahum 1:3).

> *I have loved you with an everlasting love; I have drawn you with loving-kindness.*
>
> —Jeremiah 31:3

DAY 3

We have invested (not spent!) the past two days studying God's anger as recorded in the Old Testament and as lived out in Jesus Christ. Today we will turn the lens on ourselves and see how our fits of anger compare with God's sinless anger. Recalling one temper tantrum my daughter had when she was two years old is an appropriate place to start as we begin our time together today. I don't remember what made my daughter so livid that afternoon; the years and the busyness of our lives have blurred my memory. There have been many times of anger in my own life, though, that I remember all too well. Believe me, I haven't forgotten what triggered my anger in those instances.

Write your top two pet peeves here.

_____

_____

I have more than two. I also have "triggers" that go much deeper than trivial pet peeves. **Think about a time recently when your blood pressure went through the roof. Write three words that describe how you felt in that moment.**

On day 1 of this week's study, we looked at Paul's instruction in Ephesians 4:26–27, in which he says, "'In your anger do not sin': Do not let the sun go down while you are still angry, and do not give the devil a foothold."

Read Ephesians 4:29–31. What gives the devil a "foothold"?

In verse 31, Paul lists six forms of *sinful* anger. Study their Greek translations and original definitions. Afterward, answer the questions below.

Bitterness: *pikrías*. Bitter, offensive to God. *Antonym:* joy, delight, gladness of heart.

Rage (NIV)/wrath (KJV): *thumós*. Violent motion, violent passion **of the mind**. *Thumós* is an outburst of anger, a passionate and temporary characteristic of anger.

Anger: *orgé*. Covet after, desire, a state **of mind**, quick-temperedness. *Synonym:* bitterness. *Antonym:* mildness, quietness, peace, calm, patience.

Brawling (NIV)/clamor (KJV): *kraugé.* To cry, to wail for help.

Slander (NIV)/evil speaking (KJV): *blasphemía.* Verbal abuse against someone, wounding someone's reputation by evil report, backbiting, railing, insult, hurt, irreverent. *Antonym:* reverence.

Malice: *kakía.* Wickedness as an evil habit **of the mind.** Sin, insult, injustice, spite, ill will.

Besides being forms of anger that can destroy our lives and relationships, do you find anything else that these have in common?

_____

_____

Where does anger begin?

_____

_____

At what point does it become sinful?

_____

_____

We learn what we live. Perhaps you grew up in a home filled with anger or perhaps you were victimized, hurt, and left with an anger that will not let up. **With which form of anger just described can you best identify and why?**

_____

_____

_____

_____

Aristotle said, "Anger is desire mixed with grief." What does this mean to you?

_____

_____

_____

_____

Interruptions to our well-made plans leave us feeling hurt and disappointed. The plan, or the life, we had hoped for dies right before our eyes. Something inside of us wants to die, too. The sadness we feel is grief. **When grief mixes with a desire that won't go away, what is the result?**

_____

_____

_____

_____

Anger is something we have in common with God. Sin is not. **What did Paul tell us to do with the forms of anger listed above from Ephesians 4:31?**

_____

I want to say a word to those of us who struggle with these kinds of anger. We don't need anyone to tell us that bitterness, rage, anger, brawling, slander, and malice give the devil a foothold. We know it well from experience—_painful_ experience. God wants you "to get rid of" all the destructive anger. _All of it_. But how?

In the original Greek, "to get rid of" (NIV) or "to put away from you" (KJV) is _aíro_, meaning to take up, to remove by carrying away. Do you have your seat belts buckled? I hope so, because what comes next is awesome.

Aíro is used in other places in the Bible. I want you to go there and write what you find.

Matthew 8:16–17 (The words "took up" are *"aíro."*)

_____

_____

_____

1 Peter 2:24 (The word "bore" is *"aíro."*)

_____

_____

_____

Great news! You don't have to struggle with anger any longer! You don't even have to figure out how to get rid of it! Jesus already struggled with it on the cross and *"aíro-ed"* it far from you! Jesus got rid of it, put it away *for* you and *for* me at Calvary! He literally *aíro*-ed it by carrying it away! Praise God! As He carried His cross, He removed and carried away the old you with its bitterness, rage, anger, brawling, slander, and malice! Would you like to know where it is today?

Read Colossians 2:13–14. Where was your anger last seen alive?

_____

_____

_____

"He took it away, nailing it to the cross."

It thrills our enemy, Satan, to see us fighting battles that Christ already won. That's when he gets a foothold in our lives.

We will never win the battle on our own. You don't have to live life as an angry person. Your struggle with anger today was won 2,000 years ago.

Then why does it keep raising its ugly head in our lives? Only because we allow it to do so. The moment anger awakens, we must do two things. First, we must discern whether its motive is to preserve the best and guard the welfare of that which God values, or whether its motive is the preservation of me, myself, and mine.

If anger's motive is right in God's eyes, then pray for His help and grace in expressing it without sinning. If anger's motive is self-preservation, then tackle it immediately. Ever get a spaghetti stain on your white blouse or grape juice on your Berber carpet? What was your reaction? Quick, get water, soap, and a rag! You dealt with it *immediately* if you wanted to salvage the blouse or the carpet! What happened if you didn't deal with it right away? The oils and colors soaked down deep into the fibers and caused a stain. The same is true with sinful anger. We must pounce on it immediately with the water and soap of God's Word and scrub it out with sincere prayer and repentance. If we let anger just sit there on the carpet of our heart, the fixed stain it causes will detract from the beauty of Christ in us and subtract from all that God intends for us.

"For nothing is impossible with God."
—Luke 1:37

"Blessed is she who has believed that what the Lord has said to her will be accomplished!"
—Luke 1:45

★ DAY 4

bet you're thinking, *Okay, that takes care of my anger. Now what about God's anger toward me?* Look back to day 2 of this week's study, and review what you learned. We'll pick up where we left off. We already explored *what* makes God angry; now let's find out *who* makes Him angry.

Who has provoked Him to anger with their sin? Read Romans 3:23.

_____

_____

Genesis 4 is the story of Cain and Abel. **Read Genesis 4:5–6. What emotion led to sin?**

_____

Read Genesis 4:8–12. What sin did Cain's anger lead to?

_____

What connection did Jesus explain in Matthew 5:21–22?

_____

_____

_____

Jesus equated sinful anger with murder. Why do you think this is true?

_____

_____

_____

In the end, unleashed and uncontrolled anger kills. It kills friendships, marriages, and parent-child relationships. It snuffs out joy, dreams, hopes, and potential. It poisons our prayers, butchers our beliefs, and can put an end to our fulfilling God's purpose for our lives.

Because God is holy, He can have nothing to do with sin. All sin must be punished because God is just. In Genesis 4:10–12, we learn how God punished Cain for his anger-induced sin.

What was Cain's response to God in Genesis 4:13?

_____

_____

What is God's punishment for our sins? See Romans 6:23.

_____

God knew that this sentence was too much for us to bear, too. What did God, in His great love for us, do about this? Read Romans 3:25.

_____

_____

Whom did God present?

_____

How does the Holy Spirit, through Paul, describe Jesus?

_____

_____

The New International Version of the Bible states that God presented Him "as a sacrifice of atonement." This phrase is also translated "as one who would turn aside his wrath, taking away sin."

Whose wrath would Jesus turn away from us?

_____

Read Romans 5:6–9. By what is anyone saved from God's wrath?

_____

_____

_____

How did Jesus take upon Himself the wrath of God that we deserve?

_____

_____

Read 1 Thessalonians 1:9–10. From what had these believers turned away?

_____

What had they turned toward? (Note the two things.)

_____

_____

What is the Son's name? What is the Son's role?

_____

_____

Skip over to 1 Thessalonians 5:1–4, 9. What is God's desire for us?

_____

_____

_____

Read 1 Thessalonians 5:10–11. With what message are we told to encourage one another?

_____

_____

_____

Before we trusted in Christ for our salvation, what were we? See Ephesians 2:3.

_____

On whom does God's wrath remain? Read John 3:36.

_____

_____

Praise God that we who confess with our mouths that Jesus is Lord and believe in our hearts that God raised Him from the dead (see Romans 10:9) stand secure, safe, and protected from the righteous, just, and imminent anger of God. Jesus ran interference for us and took all God's wrath on Himself. He carried (_aíro!_) our own sinful anger, nailed it to the cross to give us victory over such a potentially destructive emotion, and then endured God's anger toward our sins. **What is the result?**

Hebrews 4:16

_____

_____

Colossians 2:9–10

_____

_____

_____

O the deep, deep love of Jesus,
Spread His praise from shore to shore!
How He loveth, ever loveth,
Changeth never, nevermore!
How He watches o'er His loved ones,
Died to call them all His own;
How for them He intercedeth,
Watcheth o'er them from the throne!
                                    —Samuel Trevor Francis

✫ DAY 5

 aith in Jesus Christ is the remedy for God's wrath that we so deserve. Today, I hope you will discover that He is also the cure for your unhealthy anger as well.

Return to Ephesians 4:17–32. This portion of the Word is subtitled "Living as Children of Light" in my NIV. Another version titled it "A New Way of Thinking." On day 3 of this week, we invested considerable time focusing on verse 31. It is critical when studying Scripture to keep the instruction and truth in context. That means reading what comes before and what comes after the portion being studied. Keeping everything in context always sheds more light and gives correct understanding on the issue.

Where are we taught to be made new? Read Ephesians 4:23.

_____

Do you remember where anger begins? Look back at day 3.

_____

The instruction and commands given to us as Christians are simply impossible to carry out without a change of mind and heart. Real change in a person's outward life is unattainable unless real change has taken place inwardly first. Yesterday's homework may have been a review for some of you, or it may have been the first time some of you ever heard it. It is paramount to know first and foremost that when you believe in Christ for your salvation and right standing with God, **you are re-created in that moment in the likeness of Him. You become new in every way.** The challenge comes in learning to walk out the reality of the new you. According to God's Word, the new you also has a new way of thinking about—a new way of perceiving—the world around you, and interpreting life's events and characters.

In Ephesians 4:24, Paul tells us to "put on the new self, created to be like God in true righteousness and holiness."

Read Romans 12:2. How are we transformed?

_____

_____

_____

_____

The word "renewing" is not a one-time event. The idea is that of being constantly renewed, every day, every hour, every minute as the case may be. The saying goes, "You are what you eat." **How does this relate to the idea of being "transformed by the renewing of your mind"?**

_____

_____

_____

_____

What are you listening to, watching, thinking about as you are…

    . . . getting dressed for the day?

    . . . driving, running errands and chauffeuring children?

    . . . at the office?

    . . . at the gym?

    . . . preparing dinner?

    . . . unwinding at the end of the day?

What can you change in your daily routine to renew your mind during these times?

_____

_____

_____

_____

_____

The Cure for Destructive Anger

Freedom from destructive anger is attainable. The following six steps can bring us into that freedom:

✶ **The first step** to freedom from destructive anger is trusting in Christ's death on the cross in our place.

✶ **The second step** is recognizing that we are a new creation in Christ.

✶ **The third step** is learning the importance of continual renewal of the mind.

✶ **The fourth step** is obedience to God's Word. **So what does His Word teach us about anger management?**

Galatians 5:26

_____

_____

_____

Ephesians 5:22–24

_____

_____

_____

Ephesians 6:4

_____

_____

_____

Ecclesiastes 7:9

_____

_____

_____

✭ **The fifth step** brings closure, healing, and complete liberation. **What is it?**

Ephesians 4:32

_____

_____

To what degree are we to do so? (Just as...?)

_____

_____

_____

Forgiving others may sometimes be easier than forgiving ourselves. In order to make progress in this or any other area, we must extend to ourselves the same grace and forgiveness that we would extend to others. Only then will we be able to love our neighbor as we love ourselves.

✶ **The sixth step** in curing unhealthy anger gives us focus as we live our daily lives. We must learn to live in the present moment, in the present day, while prayerfully planning for tomorrow and staying aware that God's plan and purposes prevail every single time and are best for us. We must prioritize our to-do list and carefully choose how we will respond when angry, all with the awareness of Jesus's promised return. Ask yourself, *If Christ returns this day, can I honestly say that I have followed His plan for my life today and that I expressed His loving heart in all I said and did?*

Our self-made itineraries won't stand impregnable, but they will be carved and reshaped by God-directed winds of change. "Many are the plans in a man's heart, but it is the LORD's purpose that prevails" (Proverbs 19:21). As believers, we should acknowledge God's control even in the unexpected rearrangements of our lives, be they minor or major.

All we have is the precious gift of this very moment, nothing more. Choose to live prayerfully and willingly accept God's redirections. "The LORD Almighty has sworn, 'Surely, as I have planned, so it will be, and as I have purposed, so it will stand'" (Isaiah 14:24), and again, "What I have said, that will I bring about; what I have planned, that will I do" (Isaiah 46:11).

These promises must not frighten or frustrate us. There is tremendous peace in knowing God is in control of our times because God, by His nature, is love. He has not allowed anything in our lives to harm or to destroy us. He will not contradict His nature or His Word. We will find great release in submitting to God's minute-by-minute plan for our lives.

Time and experience have taught me that for the believer, what comes dressed as a burden is really a blessing in disguise. A new friendship, a new skill, a new confidence, and a new discovery of truth are just some of the treasures life's interruptions have delivered. Hindsight teaches me to look at surprises, hurts, and disappointments differently. Now, instead of recoiling in anger, I find myself strangely eager to go on the treasure hunt to find the blessings God has lovingly hidden for me on the road ahead.

For the believer, what comes dressed as a burden is often really a blessing in disguise.

Busyness, Burnout, and the Bible

Visit any bookstore these days and you will find no shortage of titles that address the topic of 21st-century-style fatigue and burnout. Rush through any newsstand that borders your local grocery store checkout lane and you'll have your pick of "tested and proven" remedies for stress and exhaustion. Stroll down any aisle of your neighborhood health food market and you'll discover supplements and products guaranteed to help you painlessly burn your candle at both ends—products with everything from bee pollen to shark fin. Listen long enough to any two women with supermom syndrome who are having a conversation at the grocery store, office, school, or bank and you are bound to hear them speak of how busy and overworked they are, how exhausted they are, or how underappreciated they are—or, as is more often the case, all of the above.

If the truth be known, you're struggling right now as you head into week 4 of our study together, struggling to keep your eyes open, struggling to stay focused, struggling with all the voices in your head reminding you of all the things you simply *must* do today while you sleepily sip a caffeine-loaded drink. Am I right? You are familiar with this state of being. You've lived in overdrive so long that it has become the norm. You've forgotten how it is to feel any differently. Don't worry. You're not alone. America in general is an exhausted, frenzied, sleep-deprived nation on a senseless, ruthless treadmill speeding headlong into tomorrow's to-do list. Our calendars stay so packed with so much activity that we don't even really know how tired we are. We sense that something isn't right, but we haven't had the time or energy to figure it out.

There are many reasons why women in particular are tired to the bone. Many of us are often alone in life's responsibilities and are forced to carry the load solo. Military spouses, like civilian spouses married to businessmen who travel constantly, face weeks, months, and years of keeping the home fires burning all by themselves. Many women are divorced or widowed and must hold down full-time jobs while rearing children or grandchildren alone. Then there are the countless women who live with emotionally absent, disengaged, disinterested husbands, and there are the ones who are caring for their physically ill or handicapped husbands. While these are not technically alone, they still must carry the day-to-day load of family and home atop one set of delicate shoulders.

You've lived in overdrive so long that it has become the norm.

This week we are going to downshift and pull off life's freeway to look closely at what God has said about our state of sleep deprivation and exhaustion. We are going to survey work and rest from heaven's point of view and learn how to realign our lives to find balance and a remedy for burnout.

★ DAY 1

n *enigma* is something puzzling, something hard to understand or ambiguous. The writer of the Book of Ecclesiastes saw the world as full of enigmas, full of things that seem to be without purpose or without meaning.

Turn to Ecclesiastes 2:17–23. The writer, now in the closing chapters of his own life, looks back over his yesterdays and tells us how he feels about all those years he labored, worked, and toiled. **How does he feel about all his hard work?**

_____

_____

_____

_____

_____

_____

_____

Do you carry a heavy workload? Choose three words to describe how you feel about your responsibilities today.

_____

_____

_____

Read Ecclesiastes 3:1–8. I want you to assign each of these "activities under heaven" to one of two categories: work or rest. Go verse by verse and decide whether the activity sounds more like working or resting.

WORK	REST

How many activities involved work? _____

How many activities involved rest? _____

The saying goes, "Many hands make light work"; however, shouldering burdens alone makes work so much heavier and, at times, unbearable. **Read Ecclesiastes 4:7–12.**

Which is better, toiling together or laboring alone?

_____

Why? _____

_____

_____

_____

On a scale from 1 to 10, with 1 being dog-tired-to-the-bone and 10 being the most energized, the most rested, and the most rejuvenated, plot where you feel you are today.

1 _____ 5 _____ 10

If you put yourself somewhere below 5, can you explain why you are so tired?

_____

_____

_____

_____

_____

Paul tells us in Galatians 6:9, "Let us not become weary in doing good, for at the proper time we will reap a harvest if we do not give up." With all his tent making and traveling itineraries, surely he frequently wrestled with fatigue. **What does this instruction mean to you?**

_____

_____

_____

_____

Do you think that it is possible to work without growing weary? _____

If your answer is yes, what secret have you discovered that steers you clear of burnout and its end result, fatigue-induced depression?

_____

_____

_____

_____

DAY 2 ⭐

*W*ith all the items on our endless mental to-do list, it is critical that we develop and maintain a biblical view of work. To do so, we must dig deeply into God's Word, climb up on our Father's knee, and then look at this enigma called labor from the viewpoint of the One who created it.

Take a couple of minutes and list everything you did yesterday from the time you awakened to the minute your head hit the pillow at bedtime. Don't leave anything out. Be specific. Then add to this what you have to do today. Be thorough.

Yesterday I…

_____

_____

_____

_____

_____

_____

_____

_____

_____

_____

_____

_____

_____

_____

_____

_____

_____

_____

_____

Today I…

_____

_____

_____

_____

_____

_____

_____

_____

_____

_____

_____

_____

_____

_____

_____

_____

Hope for the Home Front Bible Study

_____

_____

_____

_____

_____

Give three reasons why we work.

_____

_____

_____

If Work and Rest starred in a movie set in the Wild West, what color hat would Work be wearing, and what color horse would he be riding—black or white? _____

Based on your list of activities recorded, which is getting more screen time, the "good" guy or the "bad" guy? _____

Many of us have a wrong opinion of and approach to work. The results of an unbiblical view of work are laziness, procrastination, excuses, employment below one's potential, loss of creativity, unemployment, welfare, poverty, resentment, and depression, to name just a few.

On today's stage, *work* is considered a four-letter word for many of us. Why is this so? Can you think of anything that causes us to think this way?

_____

_____

_____

Read Genesis 1:26–28 and Genesis 2:8, 15. Where did work originate?

_____

_____

_____

Exertion in Eden seems to be a paradox in paradise, doesn't it? Yet God created man and woman *and work* on the same sixth day. You may be thinking, are you telling me that work is a *good* thing? **Read Genesis 1:31. How does God feel about work?**

_____

_____

If work is not the culprit, then why are we so weary? When did work become burdensome? Read Genesis 3, especially verses 17–19 and 23.

_____

_____

Jesus understands what it means to work hard. Jesus is the Word that became flesh and lived among us. He was virgin born and lived a sinless life, yet He lived in our fallen world and experienced everything and more that we experience, including backbreaking, exhausting work. The curse that was pronounced in Eden is the same curse under which Jesus chopped, sawed, and sanded wood in His dad's dusty carpentry shop. Jesus understands firsthand what it is to put one's sweat, blood, and tears into one's work. As the oldest son, He worked diligently alongside His parents to provide for His earthly family. At 30 years old, He worked alongside His heavenly Father as a teacher, prophet, and physician, providing for the needs of God's family by the sweat of His brow.

The following portions of Scripture paint a portrait of a tired Savior. What did Jesus do when He was exhausted?

John 4:4–6

_____

_____

Mark 4:35–39

_____

_____

Luke 5:16

_____

_____

Jesus respects and values hard-working individuals. Think about it. Did Christ call as His disciples elite gentlemen with clean hands or willing workers, some with calloused hands and dirty fingernails? Read Matthew 4:18–22 and Mark 2:13–14.

_____

_____

_____

Read Galatians 3:13. What was Jesus doing on that cross?

_____

_____

Jesus died on that cross to save our souls and to give us eternal life. Jesus said that He came that we might have eternal life after death, but also that we can know abundant life here and now. When Jesus redeemed us from the curse of the law, He also redeemed our work, our career, our calling, our responsibilities, which were under the curse! Jesus not only redeemed our souls but also redeemed God's order that was set in place at creation, including the meaningfulness and the enjoyment and the rewarding productivity of God-given work. God does not want us to "endure" the calling He has on our lives. What we do daily, minute by minute, hour by hour, is precious in the sight of God. Jesus spilled His blood, sweat, and tears so that we could once again experience labor the way the Lord, who is Love, intended it to be.

> *"I have come that they may have life,*
> *and have it to the full."*
> —John 10:10

 # DAY 3

> *Never miss a chance to rest your horse.*
> —From *A Cowboy's Guide to Life*
> by Texas Bix Bender

*a*utumn is hurricane season on America's east coast. Last fall, we Virginians got fully acquainted with one named Isabel. She threw a wet and windy tantrum across our region and blew out our power, leaving us without electricity for many days. A strange and unexpected thing happened during this time in our family. Although we had a huge mess to clean up from her tirade, Isabel taught us a very valuable lesson about balancing work and rest. When Isabel blew out our power, we got some much-needed rest! Why? We had no television, no computer, and no phone service to flicker, beep, ring, and drone on to interrupt our evenings! It was very dark and very quiet when that Indian summer sun went down. So we decided to go to bed! What a novel idea! Why didn't we think of that before? We worked hard during the daylight sawing fallen trees, dragging branches to the curbside, and helping neighbors retrieve patio furniture and garbage can lids that had frisbeed down the street. But at night we got some rest. I believe that is exactly the way God intended us to rest, to stop at the end of the day, to power down, to be still, and to *go to sleep*. It is dark at night for a good reason!

It is dark at night for a good reason!

Americans for some reason don't get it. We stay open 24/7, 365 days a year. Need milk? No worries. Just stop at Wal-Mart at 2:30 A.M. Forgot your mother-in-law's birthday? No problem. You can swing into the Super K-Mart at midnight and find her favorite cologne on sale. And as if news on the half hour, every hour, isn't enough, we struggle to stay up for the 11:00 evening news anyway, just to make sure our swollen eyes haven't missed the latest headline. We use our late night and weekend cell phone minutes to talk to distant friends and family while our kids IM (send instant messages to) their 500 best friends into the wee hours of the morning. We refuel our cars, recharge our cell phones, cool our car engines, recycle our trash, restock our refrigerators, and even insist that our babies have their naps. Yet we don't do the same for *ourselves*. We simply don't know when enough is enough. We don't know how to stop and relax anymore.

That's not God's design or desire for us. God's order of things is in perfect balance. Day and night. Summer and winter. Fall and spring. Planting and harvest. Hot and cold. Light and dark. God has designed His creation, which includes us, with the need and the opportunity for rest. He not only *made* His creation with this in mind, but He has *mandated* periods of rest.

Write out the following verses in the space provided. Underline the selected words, and then study their original Hebrew and Greek meanings.

Write out Psalm 46:10. Underline the words *be still*, *know*, and *God*.

_____

_____

_____

_____

Be still: *râphâh*. In Hebrew this word means to cease, consume, draw toward evening, to leave it alone, to let it alone.

(Wow! I have to share something amazing and beautiful here with you. One of God's names is *Yahweh Rapha*, which is where we get *râphâh*. This root word means "to mend by stitching, to cure, to heal, to repair, to thoroughly make whole." This name for God, *YHWH Rapha*, the Lord who heals, is found in Exodus 15:26. I don't know about you, but I'm glad God knows how to stitch, since my life flies apart at the seams so often!)

Know: *yâda'*. In Hebrew this word means to acknowledge, to ascertain by seeing, to recognize, to observe, to be aware, to consider, to discover.

Hope for the Home Front Bible Study

God: *elôhîm.* In Hebrew this word is the plural form of the supreme God: the Father, the Son, and the Holy Spirit.

For those of you who haven't discovered versions of the Bible that expound and include the original language and meanings the writers used and intended, I highly suggest you borrow or buy one. I recommend Zondervan's *The Amplified Bible.* These versions put meat on the bones of verses that seem too "skinny" to the English reader and give deeper understanding into the heart of the passage. Here is my own "amplified" version of the first part of Psalm 46:10:

> *Stop what you're doing, look around, recognize Elohim—the Father, the Son, the Holy Spirit—in everything happening around you, and you will be healed, be mended, be repaired by observing, considering, discovering Him and His design for your life.*

Write your own amplified version of Psalm 46:10 with the knowledge you gained from the word study above.

_____
_____
_____
_____
_____

Write out Isaiah 30:15. Underline the words *repentance,* *rest,* *saved* (or *salvation*), *quietness,* *trust,* **and** *strength.*

_____
_____
_____
_____

Repentance (NIV)/returning (KJV): *shûbâh*. In Hebrew this word means to return to the starting point.

Rest: *nachath*. In Hebrew this word means quietness.

Saved: *yâsha'*. In Hebrew this word means freed, helped, preserved, rescued, kept safe. Do you remember that we studied this word during week 1? **Whose name comes from this root word?**

_____

Quietness: *shâqat*. In Hebrew this word means to be at rest, to be still.

Trust (NIV)/confidence (KJV): *betach*. The Hebrew root word means a place of refuge, the fact and feeling of safety, assurance.

Strength: *gebûwrâh*. This Hebrew word means force, mastery, might, power. It comes from the root word *gibbôr* which means mighty one, champion, warrior. (Wow again! Another name for God is Yahweh *Gibbor*, the Lord is a Mighty Warrior!)

Write your own amplified version of Isaiah 30:15 with the knowledge you gained from the word studies above.

_____

_____

_____

_____

_____

_____

"The Lord your God is with you,
he is mighty to save.
He will take great delight in you,
he will quiet you with his love,
he will rejoice over you with singing."
—Zephaniah 3:17

DAY 4

Our family had the incredible privilege of visiting Israel in October 2000 during Sukkot, the Feast of Tabernacles. We stayed ten days, our travel being limited to Jerusalem and En Gedi due to the start of what is now called the Intifada, a sad saga of ongoing gun battles and bloodshed in the Palestinian territories of the West Bank and Gaza. One of my most special memories was experiencing two Sabbaths in Jerusalem. I hope you will enjoy these memories from my travels:

Shabbat in Jerusalem…a hush is over the city. The avenues, streets, hotels, government buildings, and markets, usually flowing and pumping with colorful, noisy cars, buses, and people, are nearly empty. Only a few taxis crawl here and there like the last ants to take cover in the anthill before a rain squall. It's so quiet in the city I can almost hear the sun shining. Didn't even have to push a button in the elevator today. The buttons for every floor stay lit up today so no one has to work, breaking the Sabbath to push one. I wanted French fries with my lunch. The room service person reminded me that no

fires can be lit today. Only cold food till sunset. Sigh.
Sabbath. What a great idea.

On the sixth day of creation God created animals, man, woman, and work. What did God do the next day? Read Genesis 2:2–3.

_____

_____

Do you think God, who has no beginning and no end, who never sleeps nor slumbers, was tired? _____

Why then do you think He rested?

_____

_____

There were other occasions when God, through His Son, set an example for us, not because it was something *He* personally needed, but because He knew *we* needed it. **What were some of the other examples He set besides His example of rest?**

Matthew 3:13–15

_____

_____

_____

John 13:1–17

_____

_____

_____

On what day did God rest? Read Genesis 2:2. _____

Although Sunday is the first day of our week, not the seventh, many Christians keep Sabbath on Sunday. Are Sundays truly restful for you?

_____

_____

What two things did God do to the Sabbath day? Read Genesis 2:3.

_____

_____

God's desire for us concerning the Sabbath is found in the fourth of the Ten Commandments. **Read Exodus 20:8–10 and answer the following:**

How are we to keep the Sabbath holy?

_____

_____

_____

Why? _____

_____

_____

Read Exodus 31:14–17. What did God call the Sabbath?

_____

_____

_____

For how long was it to be observed?

_____

_____

Why did God require that His people observe the Sabbath? (Hint: Refer to your word study on Psalm 46:10 on day 3.)

_____

_____

_____

Based on Psalm 46:10 and your knowledge of the Sabbath, what is a prerequisite to _knowing_ God?

_____

_____

_____

God honors and rewards our obedience to His Word, and He offers rewards for keeping the Sabbath holy. **Read Isaiah 58:13–14.**

What are the _ifs_ or conditions listed?

_____

_____

_____

_____

What are the results or rewards?

_____

_____

_____

For whom was the Sabbath made? Read Mark 2:27–28.

_____

What did Jesus call Himself in the verses above?

_____

The study of the meanings of numbers in the Bible always captures my attention. The number six represents incompleteness and man, man's ways, and man's efforts. The number seven is one that connotes completion, holiness, and godliness throughout the Bible.

Do you see what I see? We are to work six days and rest one day—now that is correct theology. One day of stillness, rest, quiet reflection, and worship, plus six days of labor, equals seven days…seven, the number of wholeness, completion, holiness to the Lord…a correct and balanced theology of work and rest. That's a 6 to 1 ratio of work days to rest days. Six (man) plus one equals seven (wholeness found in doing things God's way). Our part is to do our best, diligently, for six days and to be still on the seventh day. God's part is to heal us and to restore us on the one day of the week that He has set aside. Some people would say that the Sabbath was only for the Jews, yet it was part of the original perfect creation before the nation of Israel existed.

What are your thoughts?

_____

_____

_____

_____

_____

_____

DAY 5

*i*n week 1, we read, talked about, and studied the account of the Israelites at the border of Canaan in Numbers 13 and 14. We looked closely at their exaggerated fears, their lack of trust in God's ability to keep His promise, and their resulting discouragement and disobedience to Him. **Read Hebrews 3.**

What did God declare on oath concerning these unbelieving people (v. 11)?

_____

_____

_____

What is His "rest"?

_____

_____

_____

_____

Read Hebrews 4:1–11. Verse 1 states that "the promise of entering his rest still stands." Do you think then that God's rest, which the Israelites did not enter, is only referring to the physical land of Canaan promised to the Israelites? What then is His rest that still stands?

_____

_____

_____

_____

What same message did the ancient Israelites hear that we too have heard (v. 2)?

_____

_____

Why couldn't they enter God's rest (v. 6)?

_____

_____

Read Ephesians 2:8–9 for more insight into the meaning of God's rest. By what are we not saved?

_____

_____

_____

By what are we saved?

_____

_____

_____

> _Just as entering physical rest in Canaan demanded faith in God's promise, so salvation-rest is entered only by faith in the person and work of Jesus Christ._
> —NIV Study Bible footnotes for Hebrews 4:3

The Rest of the Story

It has been said that "one man's trash is another man's treasure." In light of our study this week, we could say, "one woman's exhaustion is another woman's vacation!" Each of us finds rest in different ways. For most women, leisurely shopping is a refreshing treat. For me, mall surfing is a dreaded drain.

What about you? What do you find truly relaxing? What activities really recharge your battery?

_____

_____

_____

_____

God has created us all uniquely. It makes sense then that His prescription for personal rest would be just as unique. One truth never changes: the recognition of and reliance on Jesus Christ's total sufficiency for every challenge results in God's kind of work and God's kind of rest for us. Strength to fulfill our many responsibilities is found in Christ alone. His name is Immanuel, God with us. He has promised to give us renewed strength.

> *Do you not know?*
>   *Have you not heard?*
> *The LORD is the everlasting God,*
>   *the Creator of the ends of the earth.*
> *He will not grow tired or weary,*
>   *and his understanding no one can fathom.*
> *He gives strength to the weary*
>   *and increases the power of the weak.*
> *Even youths grow tired and weary,*
>   *and young men stumble and fall;*
> *but those who hope in the LORD*
>   *will renew their strength.*
> *They will soar on wings like eagles;*
>   *they will run and not grow weary,*
>   *they will walk and not be faint.*
>   —Isaiah 40:28–31

Just as *strength* is found in Christ alone, *true rest* is found in Him alone. **According to the following Scriptures, who alone gives rest?**

Joshua 21:44

_____

_____

1 Kings 5:4

_____

_____

Psalm 62:1, 5

_____

_____

Psalm 91:1

_____

_____

What did Jesus say in Matthew 11:28? Write it here.

_____

_____

We find rest in God alone. Jesus said, "Come to Me...and I will give you rest." What does that make Jesus?

_____

_____

When her son and I were dating, my mother-in-law-to-be wisely told me: "Don't make him your coffee pot. Let him be the cream in your coffee." I don't drink coffee, but I got her message. No one person can be everything we need. It is not fair to place that expectation on anyone. God is the only one who is constant, always available, always ready to help. He is the one Husband who is always there and completely able. He is the one Father who is always home and completely interested. He is the one Friend who never deploys, disengages, or files for divorce. Let God be your *everything* …your strength for meeting the demands and finishing the hard work, your rest, your breath of fresh air, your quiet hiding place. That is the only way we can "not become weary in doing good."

Let God be your everything.

Tempted, Teased, Tantalized, and Tested

We exchanged glances across the crowded room. His deep brown eyes caught mine more than once. Oblivious to us, the other party guests moved and mingled politely as soft music and softer lamplight played between us. We couldn't ignore the attraction. A forbidden, unseen force drew us to one another.

The chemistry between us was instant and uncanny. Our glances became smiling gazes, unspoken invitations to meet, to talk, to connect, to rendezvous as soon as possible. I hoped no one around us could read our body language, especially my husband, who was engrossed in shoptalk with some colleagues. I gracefully weaved my way, nonchalantly and slowly zigzagging through the chatty crowd. I wanted a closer look at him. I wanted to give him a closer look at me.

I had seen him several times before at other get-togethers. It was lust at first sight and we both knew it. Bells chimed, cannons fired, and alarms screamed in my head the first time we were introduced. Initially, I only thought about him on occasion. Mental images of him, tall, dark, and handsome with a winsome, white-toothed smile, crept into my ordinary days. The occasional thoughts became more frequent. I found myself hoping to run into him as I ran routine errands. I caught myself wondering if he ever thought of me. It wasn't long until the innocent and the occasional gave way to unshakable, undeniable obsession. I couldn't concentrate in conversations, nor could I focus on my work. I desired him like no other man I had ever known.

Now we stood only a few feet from one another. I was afraid, sure that everyone could sense the charge of sensual electricity trying to connect us. His eyes looked into my very soul and spoke volumes in a silent, flirtatious way. I wanted desperately to get alone with him. I wanted to touch him. I wanted to hold him.

All good conscience left me for a split second. All my promises, vows, and commitments slipped out the door in one surreal, sensual moment. Faithfulness and fidelity flew out the window as I put my hand in his. I led him to a place where we could be alone, where we could throw off all inhibitions and wildly indulge our appetites. I didn't care what anyone thought anymore. I was willing to risk it all for one luscious moment with him. We slipped into an empty bedroom and locked the door behind us.

We were alone at last, breathless and giddy from our successful, clandestine escape from the boring small talk and superficial relationships in the other room. He was even more handsome up close, his skin smoother and darker than I had imagined. I fingered his face. I nibbled on his ear. He smiled. My heart fluttered and I smiled back. We were inflamed with desire for each other. We embraced, standing at the point of no return. My mind was made up. He was the one for me. No one else would ever do.

We fell on the bed, locked in each other's arms. I madly peeled off his shirt and bit him, chewing his chocolate head in ecstatic rapture. I had been wooed and won. Peter Rabbit himself, the best looking, tallest chocolate bunny on the party's buffet table, had seduced me. I inhaled him, feverishly consuming his sturdy neck, his broad shoulders, his chest, his muscular arms and legs, and even his cute little tail! Pete and I were finally one!

I lay there on the bed in the afterglow beside his tiny tinfoil shirt. I savored his one last crumb and exhaled a deep sigh of satisfaction. After a few minutes, I reemerged from the bedroom. Flushed, I smoothed my ruffled skirt and tousled hair and rejoined the party in the other end of the house. No one would ever know of our illicit affair. We had left no trail to follow. Ours was a delicious secret.

True Confections

I love chocolate. To me, it is a delicacy. From a simple Hershey's Kiss to mile-high French silk pie, it is acceptable to me in any size, shape, or recipe, morning, noon, or night. Brownies, bonbons, and black bottom ice cream pies have soothed many a frayed nerve and sweetened many a sour situation for me. I admit, the sweet and innocent cocoa bean has struck the death blow to every diet to which I ever swore allegiance.

Chocolate is the ultimate enticement, the choice seduction, the consummate calorie. It is incomprehensible to me why some folks are not tempted by melted fudge, Milky Way bars, or malt balls! They are unfazed by what fells me. Conversely, that which lures them doesn't get a second look from me. Nutty treats brimming with gooey walnuts, candied almonds, or desserts topped with peanuts simply don't stir me. Neither do doughnuts, croissants, cookies, or cakes, *unless* chocolate is somewhere in the name. But believe me, a chocolate Easter bunny isn't the only temptation to which I ever surrendered.

Not all of us are suckers for the same lollipop. One woman's aversion is the next woman's attraction. We all hunger for food, but we gravitate to diverse tastes. We all enjoy entertainment; we are mesmerized by various jesters. We all need release and relaxation; we find them at the hands of different mental masseurs that we believe will knead the painful knots out of our lives. We all need to feel secure; we try to find it in our self-made fortresses of money, materialism, and the praise of man. We all need love and acceptance; we pursue all types of lovers in search of the perfect love.

DAY 1

Certain temptations knock more loudly on my door when my husband is away. The absence of my best friend and months of mental monologue are a sure equation for turning my attention to self. Other shapes and sizes of temptations show up on my doorstep only when he is home.

At this point, the enemy launches psy-ops on me—that is, psychological operations. All sorts of sordid suggestions materialize in my brain matter, temptations targeted at my weak spots by an unseen, skilled archer. The enemy sneers: *Is **this** all there is? You deserve more than this…more enjoyment, more fulfillment, more attention, more credit than this. Everyone **else** has a peaceful, beautiful life. All their dreams are coming true. Yours aren't. Look at you. You're wasting your life following that man around the world, feeding his children, cleaning up after them day after lonely day. Packing up, packing out, and unpacking is your life story. Haven't you had enough already? I know just what you need. I can offer you some better options to the boredom, the loneliness, the stresses you so piously endure. Wanna hear a few?*

Think back over the past few days. What was your most intense battle (mental, physical, emotional) in the last 72 hours?

Hope for the Home Front Bible Study

_____

_____

_____

_____

_____

Who confronted or opposed you? Who sided with you? Were there any innocent bystanders? List all the individuals who had a part, an effect, or a voice in your battle.

_____

_____

_____

_____

_____

In 2001, Paramount Pictures released *What Women Want*, a romantic comedy starring Mel Gibson and Helen Hunt. The movie, rated PG-13 and definitely not a flick for children to see, has a premise worth pondering. After a freak accident, Nick Marshall, played by Gibson, discovers that he has an extraordinary gift: he can hear what women are thinking…every single word! I laughed and laughed!

You know, God really knew what He was doing at creation! Thank goodness, He made the merciful decision to let us keep our brain work confidential and our ponderings private!

During the recent conflict/struggle you mentioned above, were there comments and comebacks you considered spouting and dastardly deeds you deliberated that no one "heard" but you? Write three thoughts, whether right or

wrong, that traveled through your cerebrum in the heat of the battle.

_____

_____

_____

_____

_____

The devil cannot read our minds. No one is all knowing but God. King David wrote "You perceive my thoughts from afar.... Before a word is on my tongue you know it completely, O LORD" (Psalm 139:2, 4). While Satan cannot thread or untangle our thoughts, he does know how to tickle and tease them. He knows how our minds work. He knows our weaknesses, and he plays on both. He has dealt with billions of humans through the ages, from Adam and Eve right down to you and me! Yours and mine aren't the first female gray matter the devil has ever tantalized.

His "debut of deceit" is found in the Book of Genesis. **Read from Genesis 2:25 through the end of chapter 3.**

What did the woman (Eve) say in Genesis 3:13?

_____

_____

What did she say the serpent did to her?

_____

The New International Version of the Bible uses the word *deceived*. The King James Version of the Bible uses *beguiled*. Consider the following definitions from *The American Heritage*

Dictionary, third edition (New York, NY; Houghton Mifflin Company, 1994):

Deceive: "To cause to believe what is not true; mislead."
Beguile: "To deceive by guile (by treacherous cunning), to distract, divert…to amuse or delight."

The word *beguile* in the KJV of Genesis 3:13 comes from the Hebrew word *nâshâ,* which is defined as "to lead astray, to delude, to seduce mentally and morally, utterly and greatly."

According to these definitions, what was the serpent's real intent?

_____

_____

In the midst of your recent struggle, did any of your thoughts mislead you, distract you, or cause you to believe what is not true? If yes, what were some of those thoughts?

_____

_____

_____

_____

_____

_____

In Genesis 3:1, what word is used to describe the serpent?

_____

Read 2 Corinthians 11:3. By what was Eve deceived?

_____

The serpent's aim is the same today as it was in Paul's time, as well as in Eve's Eden. It was his aim in your personal battle you mentioned earlier. It is spelled out in the second part of 2 Corinthians 11:3. Write it here.

_____

_____

According to Romans 8:29, what is God's ultimate goal in our lives?

_____

_____

_____

Compare the devil's desire for us to God's goal for us. Do you see that they are two, polarized, exactly opposite motives? Based on this one comparison, do you think God ever *tempts* us? _____

> *When tempted, no one should say, "God is tempting me."*
> *For God cannot be tempted by evil, nor does he tempt*
> *anyone.… Don't be deceived, my dear brothers.*
> —James 1:13, 16

 ## DAY 2

O n Wednesday, I saw my two daughters off to school, tossed my suitcase into the back of the car, and left Virginia Beach for Pennsylvania. The Indian summer sun's reflection shimmered across the blue Chesapeake Bay. Graceful gulls glided just above the gentle white-tipped swells as I headed northeast across the Chesapeake Bay Bridge-Tunnel. My mind and the morning were clear as I sang along to my favorite praise songs all the way up Virginia's eastern shore. Prize-winning pumpkins, bright, bushy mums, and drying cornfields splashed autumn's palette of orange, yellow, and gold across the coastal landscape. And God was near. I sensed Him next to me, enjoying my childlike delight in His fall décor.

On Thursday, I was the guest speaker at a women's retreat. The ladies, mostly Army wives from Carlisle Barracks, laughed and cried as I delivered the messages God had given to me just for them. His Word, an accurate, timely, and sharp sword, pierced their hearts. We all left that hilltop retreat refreshed, encouraged, and praising Him. And God was near. The preparation had been so time- and energy-consuming and challenging. The journey had been costly and long. I felt His pleasure, His approval of my obedience.

On Friday, I made the return trip home. The sunny day glistened brilliantly. The day and I were lit up with God's glory inside and out, a perfect conclusion to a perfect journey…until the minute I walked through my back door. Sticky, blotchy dishes decorated every counter and end table. Smelly socks and shoes were strewn here and there. The phone rang. Daughter #1, stranded at the mall, had lost track of time and needed a ride home NOW in order not to derail her Friday night social calendar. Daughter #2 had unexpectedly brought friends home from school and needed to be at THE sleepover of the year in just ten minutes.

After what felt like "Mr. Toad's Wild Ride" through rush hour traffic, our daughters were safely delivered to their destinations. My husband and I, in great need of couple time, headed out to dinner. I eagerly began to tell him about all the wonderful things

God had done in and through me at the retreat. My belly laughter and animated storytelling were interrupted with an uninvited announcement from him that he'd soon be returning to the conflict in Iraq for a third time. I almost vomited.

Hot tears filled my eyes. My appetite went out the window. My face tightened. My lips thinned in anger. How could this be? How could I, who had been soaring "on wings of eagles," be shot down so quickly? My joy in the Lord plummeted to the hard earth in a death spiral as Mark tried to explain. Our romantic wonderland quickly dissolved into World War III. The waitress noticed and brought our check prematurely. We rode home in sickening silence. What in the world had happened? Just moments before, I had been high on heaven's goodness. Now I was being stared down by the ravenous, growling hounds of hell.

I am comforted to know that my Savior understands the roller coaster ride I experienced that day. **Read Matthew 3:13 through 4:11. What had preceded Jesus's fasting and temptation in the wilderness?**

_____

_____

_____

_____

_____

The devil, Satan, came growling and nipping at Jesus on the heels of a "mountaintop" experience in Jesus's life. What is the devil called in Matthew 4:3?

_____

The Israelites were expecting a certain kind of Savior, one who would meet their physical needs on demand and at their whim, one who would perform awesome public miracles to deliver them immediately from their oppressive enemies, and one who would finally and completely conquer and claim all of the Promised Land, fulfilling God's word to them. The devil was aware of the people's expectations.

What was the first suggestion the devil made to Jesus after He had fasted 40 days?

_____

_____

Can you think of a time in His earthly ministry when Jesus used His supernatural powers to satisfy His own needs or to rescue Himself?

_____

_____

What was the devil's second suggestion?

_____

_____

Can you think of a time in Jesus's life or ministry when He displayed His divine strength and godlikeness in a showy, sensational, prideful manner?

_____

_____

What was the devil's third suggestion?

_____

_____

"All the kingdoms of the world and their splendor" are promised to the Lord Jesus in the Old and New Testaments. Throughout history, what has been the world's stance concerning Christ's sovereign Kingdom rule? Read Psalm 2:2.

_____

_____

_____

There is still much work to be done before Christ reigns over the kingdoms of this earth, a truth our Savior and Satan both knew; however, the devil, Satan, wanted Christ to compromise to get the package deal earlier…before the Lord would die and be raised from the dead. **Why do you think this was so?**

_____

_____

_____

Each time the devil tempted Jesus, how did our Lord respond to him?

_____

_____

All three of Jesus's responses are references from one book in the Old Testament; He chose to quote from Deuteronomy:

> *Man does not live on bread alone but on every*
> *word that comes from the mouth of the LORD.*
> —Deuteronomy 8:3

> *Do not test the LORD your God.*
> —Deuteronomy 6:16

*Fear the L*ORD *your God, serve him only.*
—Deuteronomy 6:13

What did the devil do after Jesus responded the third time with Scripture? Read Matthew 4:11.

_____

_____

In the most stressful and critical moment thus far of His earthly life, Jesus responded to what must have seemed the easier way to His foretold reign with three brief sentences found in just one book of the Old Testament. Jesus knew every word of the 39 Old Testament books as well as every word of the yet-to-be-written New Testament.

Why do you suppose this private account of the temptation of Christ and His responses is public record for us?

_____

_____

_____

_____

_____

_____

Jesus demonstrated to us the unique, life-giving, potent, overcoming power of the Word of God. Every second that we commit to hiding His Word in our hearts is an empowering, equipping investment of our time. Only God knows what struggles and devilish schemes wait around the bend for us. He has given us His unchanging Word to face those temptation-filled days confidently and victoriously, just as His Son did.

What are the first four recorded words (NIV) of Satan when he approached Eve in the form of a serpent? See Genesis 3:1.

_____

_____

In the face of each temptation, Christ chose to believe and to obey His Father's Word. Then, the devil left Him "until an opportune time," according to Luke 4:13.

Who came to Christ's aid in that moment? See Matthew 4:11 again. _____

Who comes to our aid when we are tested and tempted? Read 1 Peter 5:8–11.

_____

_____

In that restaurant Friday night, in the deafening crossfire of anger, disappointment, and seeming injustice, God was near. Just as He had been there in all my recent successes and triumphs, He was there on that battlefield beside me. Likewise, He is there in your war zones, too. Look to Him. Follow Christ's example and watch Satan skedaddle.

> _Because he himself_ [Jesus] _suffered when he was tempted, he is able to help those who are being tempted."_
> —Hebrews 2:18

DAY 3

*M*y daughters and I are a lot alike. Sometimes this is great. We find the same jokes hilarious, the same clothes classy, the same subjects interesting, and the same desserts irresistible. Sometimes our similarities are seeds for conflict. Too often I see in them the same attitudes, weaknesses, and habits I despise in myself. Usually I can keep my cool. Other times we butt our stubborn, hard heads and sparks fly! It doesn't take much for kin to become kindling, does it?

I remember one spring day not long ago. I had opened most of the windows throughout the house and invited the refreshing breeze inside. For some reason, Jenna and I couldn't get on the same page that day. She pushed my buttons and I pushed hers. Finally, I couldn't take it any more. I lost control of my volume and my vocabulary and let her have it. As I hollered, my voice filled my house and overflowed into the neighborhood through my open windows. All my neighbors, who also had their windows open, had no choice but to hear my ugly, emotional explosion in stereo. Jenna quietly walked away to her room. I stood there horrified at what had spilled from my heart and mouth.

Those who live with us know us best. They know the real deal, don't they? There's no pulling the wool over the eyes of our closest kin and friends. They witness the good, the bad, and the ugly in our lives on a daily basis. I wish it weren't so, but it seems consistent across the board that the ones we love the most are the ones we wound most deeply by our poisonous words and self-centered reactions.

Read Romans 7:14–23. Do you know that unbelievers who do wrong, who hurt others, who commit crimes *have no other choice* *but to do wrong,* to hurt others, and to commit crimes? They can't help it!

Paul was writing about those who are under the Law which God gave to Moses. Every person since Moses's time was born under that perfect Law. Apart from a relationship with God through faith in God's Son, Jesus Christ, we are held accountable to that standard of utter perfection. **Read Romans 6:15–21, and write your thoughts.**

_____

_____

Who has achieved perfection and attained God's approval by keeping all the rules? Read Romans 3:9–22.

_____

Praise God! One man, Jesus Christ, the sinless Son of God, arrived at just the right time in history to address this very problem and to meet *our deepest need...our need to be freed from our slavery to sin so that we could live the life of victory God intended for us to live* daily, minute by minute, hour by hour.

To whom does God give this kind of righteousness? Read Romans 3:21–29.

_____

_____

It's pretty obvious that many believers miss this important point and continue to live in sin and in defeat. Too many Christians continue to carry a weighty load of guilt and resign themselves to a life of being constantly conquered in areas of personal weakness. This doesn't have to be the case!

Read Romans 7:24 through 8:2. Are we still slaves to sinful thoughts, desires, and actions?

_____

_____

_____

How do you know?

_____

_____

_____

_____

We are no longer to lie shackled to our inability to keep all the Law! Christ took care of that on the cross and gives to us who believe and trust Him two priceless and true realities:

✵ **Perfection in the eyes of Almighty God**—"By one sacrifice he has made perfect forever those who are being made holy" (Hebrews 10:14).

✵ **The ability to say no to wrong things**—"For the grace of God that brings salvation has appeared to all men. It teaches us to say 'No' to ungodliness and worldly passions, and to live self-controlled, upright and godly lives in this present age, while we wait for the blessed hope—the glorious appearing of our great God and Savior, Jesus Christ, who gave himself for us to redeem us from all wickedness and to purify for himself a people that are his very own, eager to do what is good" (Titus 2:11–14).

What a great contrast to Paul's description of the one who lives apart from God in total, constant, unrelenting defeat! Because of the cross of Christ and His Holy Spirit living in us, we now have a choice when it comes to sin!!

"So if the Son sets you free, you will be free indeed."
—John 8:36

Even with all the divine power and promises at our disposal, we believers still do wrong and need God's grace and forgiveness every single day.

As soon as I realized my tantrum had outdone hers, I went to Jenna and apologized, asking for her to forgive my embarrassing display of two-year-old behavior, adult-style. I asked her for a second chance. A little while after I lost my cool with her, she returned and handed to me a 3-by-5 index card she had colored and folded into thirds. In purple marker, she had written on the front, "Second Chance Card." On the back, she had written, "It's OK, Mommy." She said that I could use it anytime I needed it.

It's been years since that awful moment. I carry that index card in my wallet at all times, where I see it often. It reminds me that God is a God of second chances, of third chances, of fourth chances.... Why? Because He is LOVE. He paid for all those second chances with the blood of His Son, Jesus. The cross of Christ is God's "Second Chance Card" to us. And as long as I never take His sacrifice lightly or for granted, I can take out this sacred "Second Chance Card," the cross, and use it as often as needed.

If we claim to be without sin, we deceive ourselves
and the truth is not in us. If we confess our sins,
he is faithful and just and will forgive us our sins
and purify us from all unrighteousness.
—1 John 1:8–9

He is the One who is making us holy. Not we ourselves! That's His department. Our job is to grow in understanding and knowledge so as to grow in our obedience to Him.

I carry Jenna's card in my wallet wherever I go. More importantly, I carry God's Word in my heart wherever I go. Not only does His Word disarm and silence Satan, but it also reminds me that I am no longer a slave to anyone or to anything that aims to tempt, mislead, hurt, or destroy me, and that I belong to Jesus Christ for always.

> *Whenever our hearts condemn us…God is*
> *greater than our hearts, and he knows everything.*
> —1 John 3:20

> *No, in all these things we are more than conquerors*
> *through him who loved us.*
> —Romans 8:37

DAY 4

*J*ust about the time I learned to let go of my husband and to trust God with *his* life and well-being each time he deployed or went to war, God turned up the heat. I guess there is still a lot of dross in this nugget of gold.

After 20 years of entrusting my *mate* to God's plan, He is asking me to trust Him with my *son*, too! Our handsome Josh left home for college to attend Virginia Tech this year, enrolled in the university's Corps of Cadets Navy ROTC program, and aspires to be the best US Marine there ever was. Okay, Lord, You have my full attention again.

What is most difficult for you to let go, to put totally in God's hands? What or whom are you wrestling to hang on to that God has told you to release to Him completely?

_____

_____

_____

_____

What was Abraham's dearest treasure on earth? Read Genesis 22:1–19.

_____

What's yours?

_____

_____

_____

The KJV of Genesis 22:1 is translated as "And it came to pass after these things, that God did tempt Abraham, and said unto him, Abraham: and he said, Behold, here I am." **Does any word in this verse puzzle you? What is it?**

_____

Whoa! The word "tempt" threw me off, too! Doesn't James 1:13, 16 say that "When tempted, no one should say, 'God is tempting me.' For God cannot be tempted by evil, nor does he tempt anyone.... Don't be deceived, my dear brothers"? But right there in Genesis 22:1, it plainly states that "God did *tempt* Abraham."

It is important to note that the KJV's *tempt* is from the Hebrew word *nâçâh*. It means "to test, to prove, to try...to test the quality of someone or something through a demonstration of stress...to refine." It is a word for proving the integrity, the purity of the one being tested.

Compare the definition of *nâçâh* to the Hebrew word for *beguile* and *deceive* which is *nâshâ* (from day 1 this week), and means "to lead astray, to delude, to seduce mentally and morally, utterly and greatly." *Nâçâh* and *Nâshâ* sound so similar but beat with two very different hearts. The KJV uses the word *tempt* for two very different original Hebrew words, confusing English readers who understand "tempt" to connote the idea of deceit or ill will. This is an excellent example of the importance of studying the Word of God, digging deeply and unearthing treasures such as this. This discovery is so liberating to me, giving me greater understanding and a better knowledge of the heart of the God I serve.

What was God's motive in testing Abraham? Read Genesis 22:12.

_____

_____

_____

_____

_____

Abraham entered into a covenant relationship with God. It is recorded in Genesis 15, where "Abram believed the LORD, and he credited it to him as righteousness" (Genesis 15:6). At that time, God promised Abraham that "a son coming from [his] own body would be [his] heir," that his descendants would be as many as the stars in the heavens, and that He would give to those descendants "this land, from the river of Egypt to the great river, the Euphrates—the land of the Kenites, Kenizzites, Kadmonites, Hittites, Perizzites, Rephaites, Amorites, Canaanites, Girgashites and Jebusites" (Genesis 15:4–5, 18–21). When Isaac was only eight days old, his father Abraham circumcised him and dedicated him to the Lord. All of God's promises were wrapped up in one, tiny, baby blue blanket!

As Abraham's knife reflected the morning sun over Mount Moriah, God drew Abraham's attention to a ram caught in the thicket. God had provided the necessary sacrifice.

What did Abraham call that place? See Genesis 22:14.

_____

_____

_____

While God does not tempt anyone, we know that He tests us. God tests us to see if there is anything or anyone we would withhold from Him. Anyone or anything that we would withhold from God is more important to us than God Himself. And that is, quite plainly, idol worship. To withhold someone or something from the perfect will of God means to disregard, to ignore, or to overlook God's right or lordship, His sovereignty in all things.

Write Proverbs 3:5–6

_____

_____

_____

_____

_____

_____

_____

What does "in all your ways acknowledge Him" mean to you?

_____

_____

_____

When we acknowledge the Lord, His supremacy, His perfect wisdom, His unchanging love, His unlimited power, His rich goodness and graciousness in all our ways, in all our cares and concerns, in all our loved ones' lives, then we, too, can confidently call that place "The Lord Will Provide," just as Abraham did that day at Moriah.

Return to today's first question: **What is most difficult for you to let go, to put totally in God's hands?** The husband, the child, the talent, the passion, the goal that we try to keep out of God's reach will inevitably be the place of testing. The reason is that God wants our whole heart. Jesus said, "Where your treasure is, there your heart will be also" (Matthew 6:21).

I want you to write in large letters across your answer to today's first question **"The Lord will provide"** and believe in your heart that He has. He will credit it to your account as righteousness.

DAY 5

_t_he Bible is a 66-book tale of testing and temptation from cover to cover. We could camp out on this subject for years and not exhaust the stories of men, women, and children whom God tested and Satan tempted. Some came through the heat with flying colors, like Abraham, Job, Esther, Ruth, Noah, Mary, and, of course, our Savior, Jesus. Others failed the test and caved in to the tempter, such as Eve, Saul, Rehoboam, Judas, and Ananias and Sapphira. We can learn volumes of truth from each one's life and choices.

Read Hebrews 12:1–11 and answer the following:

What are we to do with sin and hindrances (v. 1)?

_____

_____

Where are our eyes to be fixed (v. 2)?

_____

Why did Jesus endure the cross and all its temptations (v. 2)?

_____

_____

Why are our eyes to be fixed on Jesus (v. 3)?

_____

_____

Whom does the Lord *nâçâh* (discipline, test, refine, prove) (vv. 4–7)?

_____

_____

Why does God *nâçâh* (discipline, test, refine, prove) us (v. 10)?

_____

_____

What does God's testing and discipline produce in our lives (v. 11)?

_____

_____

_____

> *Consider it pure joy, my brothers, whenever you face trials of many kinds, because you know that the testing of your faith develops perseverance. Perseverance must finish its work so that you may be mature and complete, not lacking anything.... Blessed is the man who perseveres under trial, because when he has stood the test, he will receive the crown of life that God has promised to those who love him.*
>
> —James 1:2–4, 12

In *Hope for the Home Front*, I underscore the importance of knowing who the enemy is, exposing that enemy, and engaging that enemy. Fill your tea cup; find a comfortable place on the couch. Enjoy this excerpt from the chapter entitled "Tempted: Absence Makes the Heart Go Wander":

Engaging the Enemy

My husband is not the only soldier in this family. I, too, am enlisted in the ranks. My battles, however, belong not to this nation, but to the Lord, "For the battle is not yours, but God's" (2 Chronicles 20:15). While Mark invades tangible enemy turf by sea, air, and land, I engage the invisible opposition on my knees. Because my Commander knows how brutal the battlefield of temptation can be, He has issued combat gear, divinely designed for my spiritual, physical, and emotional protection.

Before my feet hit the floor, I am wise to dress daily for war. Ephesians 6 inventories the protective gear at my disposal:

> *Therefore put on the full armor of God, so that when the day of evil comes, you may be able to stand your ground, and after you have done everything, to stand. Stand firm then, with the belt of truth buckled around your waist, with the breastplate of righteousness in place, and with your feet fitted with the readiness that comes from the gospel of peace. In addition to all this, take up the shield of faith, with which you can extinguish all the flaming arrows of the evil one. Take the helmet of salvation and the sword of the Spirit, which is the word of God.*
> —Ephesians 6:13–17

If I hastily start my day, entering the war zone with just one piece of armor loosely fitted, unkempt, or missing, my foe will undoubtedly target the vulnerable vital part. His prowess guarantees a bull's-eye. The arrow pierces and I, a wounded warrior, am crippled, unable to stand "against the devil's schemes" (Ephesians 6:11). Then, throughout my day, I fight ineffectively, suffer multiple injuries, and frantically limp in retreat from his onslaught. At the same time, my family and friends experience heavy casualties because I am rendered incompetent to hold the line and fight alongside them.

Defeat is avoidable when I wisely clothe myself in the armor God offers. Once I have slipped on my helmet and boots, tightened my belt and breastplate, and raised my shield, I am protected from any toxic spears Satan may hurl at me. A trained soldier doesn't just stand unarmed in the crossfire. A true warrior grasps a deadly weapon and sounds the charge. God arms us for this advance by giving us the sword of the Spirit, His powerful Word, the only offensive weapon listed in His inventory.

"The word of God is living and active. Sharper than any double-edged sword, it penetrates even to dividing soul and spirit, joints and marrow; it judges the thoughts and attitudes of the heart" (Hebrews 4:12). Jesus even demonstrated proper handling of this weapon for us when He was confronted by the tempter at the beginning of His earthly ministry. Jesus met all three temptations with Scripture, the truth all believers have at their disposal. Our arsenals are full of heavenly hand grenades, godly guns, master missiles, and all kinds of almighty artillery with which we can disarm, disintegrate, and defeat all the hostile armies that flank us.

Defeat is avoidable when I wisely clothe myself in the armor of God.

Each time temptation becomes tantalizing, I must claim God's every promise. "God is faithful; he will not let you be tempted beyond what you can bear. But when you are tempted, he will also provide a way out so that you can stand up under it" (1 Corinthians 10:13). I then must obey His every word and rely on Him to meet my every need. He says, "My grace is sufficient for you, for my power is made perfect in weakness" (2 Corinthians 12:9). And again, "My God will meet all your needs according to his glorious riches in Christ Jesus" (Philippians 4:19).

When I haven't trusted His ability to meet my needs and met them in my own way, I have found Him "faithful and just to forgive" me every time (1 John 1:9). But the times I do choose to trust Him to meet every need—whether a need for release, refueling, or redirection—I find Him faithful to reward me beyond all my expectations. Each time I turn from entertaining adulterous imaginations, God pours out His blessings onto my marriage until my relationship with my husband overflows with oneness, excitement, and fulfillment. Each time I deny the desire to drown my frustrations in alcohol, God intoxicates me with His joy, His fullness, His presence. When I take God at His word, shunned idleness becomes empowered productivity; dangerous self-confidence becomes a dance of dependence in which He alone is the Partner who leads.

As I trust God, boredom becomes blocks of freed-up time to serve others, to pursue other avenues for ministry, volunteerism, and/or continued education. God's grace transforms loneliness into the call and opportunity to grow closer to Him, to be still and to listen for His voice to comfort and guide my heart. Loneliness becomes a reason to meet and serve my neighbors and to make time for new and old friends. God curbs my sexual appetite so I can redirect the energies into penning terrific love letters to my husband, putting together outrageous care packages for him, and preparing creative, unforgettable homecomings for him.

When I am exhausted, I am learning to lean on Him, to put my head back without guilt, and to rest in the Lord. I'm learning to be very specific in my prayers and requests of Him for help and rest. Specific prayers get specific answers when prayed according to His will. When anger raises its ugly head, I tell God about it now, instead of suppressing it or exploding. In order not to "let the sun go down on my anger" and thus give Satan a foothold, I just exercise harder, praise God louder, run faster, do more weight sets, and turn up the volume and dance with abandonment to de-stress in the privacy of my living room!

I see handsome men in every direction on every US military base. Pilots in flight suits oozing with Tom Cruise appeal, Marines

Hope for the Home Front Bible Study

in those attractive red athletic shorts, and a well-built Naval officer in his choker whites win my double take. There is nothing sinful about my admiring a man's appearance or physique. Prolonged admiration, though, easily gives way to lust in the heart of a "WestPac Widow" or a geographical bachelorette. I am learning to practice a form of "chastity of the eyes" and, by God's strength, to treat younger men as brothers in the Lord and older men, no matter how handsome, as fathers, in all purity—*even those who are more tempting than Peter Rabbit.*

God's Heart: The Place I Call Home

dorothy said it best. Closing her eyes, clutching her terrier, Toto, and clicking her enchanted, sparkling shoes, she half chanted, half prayed the truth every heart knows: "There's no place like home, there's no place like home, there's no place like home." We yearn with her, there at the end of her yellow-brick road, to return to that familiar place of hearth and home, to retreat to that place of residence where we are rooted and recognized.

Dorothy's mantra is a dilemma for those of us whose lives have arced into the mobile 21st century. Very few of us live in our childhood home with Aunty Em to look after us. We live in a world that's always in motion, always on the move. Life is accelerated in our drive-through culture where money and meaning change hands from morning to midnight every day in faceless, drive-up windows across America. Life is convenient, yet cold, in this country where the average Americans change addresses 12 to 13 times in their lifetime. That's twice as many moves as the British and four times as many as the Irish. Even without a change of address, most Americans move their church membership every four years and jump into a new job 9 to 12 times between high school graduation and heading into retirement. In one or two generations, our parents' loosely knit globe has gone from comfy to cramped in the shrinking heat of high tech. Cellular phones, CNN, and the

Internet offer us a network that seems to need no family ties and no home base.

We had recently wrapped up another PCS (permanent [ha!] change of station)—our *tenth* move in 17 years. By my calculations, that's one move for every 1.7 years, just a few months longer than any address forwarding order and five times as frequent as average American transience. About the time our mail catches up to us, we pop like fleas to our next destination.

None of our moves have been easy or convenient. Whose are? All have involved hundreds of boxes, thousands of miles, and one economy-size bottle of Motrin. All have been cross-country and/or transoceanic moves, never next door or around the corner.

Moving is a way of life for military families. The Outbound/ Inbound HHG (household goods) office phone number and 1,000 copies of our new orders are things we government gypsies never leave home without. Most of us roll up our bed mats, extinguish the camp fires, strap our swinging, clanging pots and pans to the overloaded cart, and move on about every three to four years. That means we win the nation's Nomad Award, hands down.

Before moving vans and corrugated cardboard, we were known as camp followers, the soldiers' wives and children who moved with the army, making meals and mending men along the way. Technology has changed everything for the troops except their transience; therefore, we are still on the march with our service members, feeding and fixing them for the front lines.

"There's no place like home." True. That is, if one has a home. Homelessness in America is a hot topic these days. In one-tenth of a second, Yahoo.com provided me 345,000 resources on this subject! According to Tommy G. Thompson, Secretary of the US Department of Health and Human Services, 600,000 Americans are homeless on any given night. In his 2003 report on homelessness in America, Mr. Thompson categorized the homeless into three groups: the *temporarily* homeless, the *episodically* homeless, and the *chronically* homeless.

Thankfully, most of us have never had to sleep in a park, under a bridge, or along a city sidewalk, but I believe we have all at one time or another fit into one of Mr. Thompson's three categories, *spiritually speaking*. All of us have experienced a form of homelessness as we have tried to keep pace with the demands of life in the new millennium.

I believe that there is a greater epidemic than homelessness in America, and that is *homelessness of the heart*, that restless, disconnected, empty vulnerability we all encounter in today's uncertain and ever-changing world.

 ## DAY 1

*P*roverbs 3:33 is an appropriate place for us to begin our study this week. Read it in your own Bible and then write the verse below.

_____

_____

_____

_____

In your own words, describe the difference between a house and a home.

_____

_____

_____

In the Proverbs verse you just wrote, underline the following words: *curse, house, wicked, blesses, home*, and *righteous/ just*. Study each word's original Hebrew meaning below.

Curse: *meerah.* From *'arar*, meaning to execrate, to bitterly curse. (*The American Heritage Dictionary*, third edition, defines *execrate* as "to protest vehemently against, denounce, loathe, abhor.")

House: *bayith.* A house in all its applications, especially a family or household, (extended) family, (clan). From the root word *"banah,"* meaning to build, literally and figuratively; to obtain children.

Wicked: *rasha.* Morally wrong, condemned, guilty, ungodly.

Blesses: *barak.* To kneel (in this case, in an act of adoration, to congratulate, to bless abundantly and altogether).

Home (NIV)/habitation (KJV): *navah.* From the root word, *navah*, meaning to rest, as at home, implying the idea of beauty. At home, implying satisfaction; comely, pleasant place. This can apply to God's temple, man's residence, a pasture for flocks, and a den for animals.

Just: *tssadiyq.* From the root word *tasdaq*, meaning to be right in a moral, cleansed, clear sense.

According to the definitions and synonyms of the words above, what is the difference between a house and a home?

_____

_____

_____

During week 2 we discovered that unhealthy fear, the first recorded human emotion, sent Adam and Eve scurrying into the shrubs right on the heels of their prohibited picnic. We saw in week 3 that history's first recorded murder clung tightly to the skirts of self-centered anger. Likewise, homelessness is often a result of sin.

What was mankind's first home? Read Genesis 2:8, 15.

_____

Describe Adam and Eve's first home as pictured in the following verses:

Genesis 1:29–30

_____
_____
_____

Genesis 2:9

_____
_____
_____

Genesis 2:10

_____
_____
_____

Genesis 2:19–20

_____
_____
_____

Hope for the Home Front Bible Study

Genesis 2:25

_____

_____

_____

Eve sinned, and then invited her hubby to do the same. Their eyes "were opened" and they ran and hid from God. **What happened after the boy/girl blame game and God's resulting judgments on the devil, delivery, and the dirt? Read Genesis 3:22–24.**

_____

_____

_____

What was _the cause_ of this primary problem of homelessness?

_____

_____

_____

Homelessness, whether of house or heart, was sin's first stamp on society. Need more evidence? **Read Genesis 4:1–16.**

Why did God punish Cain (v. 8)?

_____

_____

_____

What was the consequence of Cain's action (vv. 10–12)?

_____

_____

_____

What did God say Cain would be (v. 12)?

_____

What did Cain have to leave (v. 16)?

_____

Where did Cain wander to and settle (v. 16)?

_____

Are you still not convinced of the association between homelessness and sin? A man named Noah was born nine generations after Adam. He drove the first moving van! Instead of "Two Men and a Truck," it was "Two of Every Creature and a Whole Lot of Muck!" **Read Genesis 6:5–22.**

What was the condition of the world in Noah's day (vv. 5, 11–12)?

_____
_____
_____
_____
_____
_____

What did God decide to do about this (vv. 7, 13, 17)?

_____
_____
_____
_____
_____
_____

While God spared Noah and his family, what did Noah have to give up?

_____

_____

Was Noah's homelessness the result of his sin or the sins of others?

_____

DAY 2

*i*n His mercy, God allowed Noah to weigh anchor and float safely on top of the deadly floodwaters that silenced all else. For more than a year, Noah and his family shared temporary quarters with countless creatures inside a noisy, smelly zoo. That makes all our temporary lodging arrangements pale in comparison, doesn't it? This was man's biggest PCS (permanent change of station) to date!

Someone was there to meet Noah and his family when they arrived at their destination. Who was it? Read Genesis 8:15.

_____

God tells us that He goes ahead of His children. When the ark finally rested atop Mt. Ararat and the waters receded, God said to Noah, "Come out of the ark, you and your wife and your sons and their wives" (Genesis 8:16). God was there to meet them when they arrived at their new home. Whether it is Mt. Ararat or Iceland or Timbuktu, I believe He does the same for all of His own.

Noah's great (x10) grandson was Abram. God made a promise to Abram in Genesis 12:7 and in Genesis 13:14–17. What was it?

_____

_____

_____

I would have started surveying the land, staking the perimeters, felling trees, and pouring cement foundations so I could settle down right then and there! Yet Scripture tells us that Abram lived a different kind of lifestyle than this.

As a military family we have lived in one-story motels with a one-local-channel TV and no maid service, a 49-story Hilton with 200 cable channels and complimentary room service, and every type of temporary lodging in between.

In what did Abram live? Read Genesis 12:8; 13:3; and 13:18.

_____

_____

What did God say the temporary living arrangements would be for Abram's descendants? See Genesis 15:13.

_____

_____

For how long? _____

God's original plan for us was a perfect home in paradise. Sin changed all that, but God, in His love and grace, promised a place His people could call "home" forever. Not only did He give it to them, He led them to it.

How did God do this? Read Exodus 13:21–22.

_____

_____

_____

When my youngest daughter was about two years old, her brother, sister, and I visited my mom and grandmother in Kannapolis, North Carolina. We all decided to visit my uncle in Raleigh. The plan was that Mom and Grandmother would follow us in their car for the day trip. Not even a half mile from my grandmother's driveway, my toddler, Jenna, unbuckled her seat belt and began bouncing around in the back seat.

I had to pull over into the nearest parking lot to secure her again. She wiggled and squirmed, protested and cried, but I firmly insisted that she stay buckled and in her seat. I returned to the driver's side, put the car in drive, and waved to my mom and grandma behind us, who were smiling sweetly and nodding with matriarchal understanding.

Before my car's tires had rolled one complete rotation, Jenna was climbing freely around in the back seat again. I stopped again (as did Mom and Grandmother), caught her by the elastic waist of her pull-up diaper, and plopped her back in her seat—this time dispersing more discipline and disapproval than before.

Ever read James Dobson's _The Strong-Willed Child_? Well, Jenna could have been his sole inspiration that day. Would you believe that I had to stop and go and stop and go _15 times_ in that one parking lot to discipline and buckle up my baby?! Once we finally made it to the interstate, what should have been an uneventful three-hour drive became a six-hour showdown due to all the necessary and unpleasant pullovers. Our two-car caravan did more stopping and readjusting than driving that day. We saw more of the road's shoulder than anything else. I could have ignored her and arrived at our destination on schedule, but I was determined to win.

A similar thing happened when God's people were "in diapers," too. A trip from Egypt to Canaan that should have taken a couple of weeks to complete took much, much longer due to His kids' disobedience and hardheadedness.

How long did this million-tent caravan have to keep "pulling over" on the highway toward home? Read Deuteronomy 2:7.

_____

Can you think of a time in your own life when you had to wait longer than expected for something you desired? What was it?

_____

_____

_____

Why were your plans delayed?

_____

_____

_____

_____

Again, God was merciful. Although they were delayed due to their disobedience, God never left them. He was determined to win...for their good and for the good of His name. He even gave Moses instructions for building a place for Himself to live right there in the middle of all their tents.

Hope for the Home Front Bible Study

Read Exodus 25:8–9. What did God call this place in verse 8?

_____

What did God call it in verse 9? _____

Let the following definitions enrich your understanding of both the *sanctuary* and the *tabernacle*.

Sanctuary: *miqdash*. A consecrated (holy) thing or place, a hallowed part; sacred because it was the place where God dwelled among His people; metaphorically used to refer to a place of refuge.

Tabernacle: *mishkan*. From *shakhan*, meaning residence; the physical and symbolic representation of God's presence among His people, portable and fully mobile.

God gave Moses very specific instructions for constructing His tabernacle. The directions for everything—from the curtains, furniture, and articles of worship inside to the bronze altar and basin outside, the placement of the tabernacle's entrance, and the shape and size of the courtyard—were completely and exactly spelled out to a T (no pun intended) (Exodus 25–31 and 35–40).

The Bible tells us that after Moses finished the work, something happened. What was it? Read Exodus 40:34–38.

_____
_____
_____
_____
_____

God was on and in the earthly tabernacle from that day until King Solomon completed the temple in Jerusalem. God consecrated this temple and put His name there forever, saying, "My eyes and my heart will always be there" (1 Kings 9:3). Later, because Israel and her rulers turned away from the Lord, Solomon's temple was burned to the ground by the Babylonians (Jeremiah 52:12–23). After 70 years of captivity, Cyrus, Persia's king who had conquered Babylon, gave the Jews permission to return to Jerusalem to rebuild God's temple (Ezra 1).

How did the Israelites respond when the new temple's foundation was laid? Read Ezra 3:12–13.

_____

_____

The older people grieved because they, unlike their children and grandchildren, had seen the beauty and the glory of the first temple of the Lord. God heard their hearts and, in His time, responded.

Girlfriend, I hope you are buckled in! **Now read John 1:14, then write this whole verse below.**

_____

_____

_____

_____

You have my permission to unbuckle yourself and bounce with joy all over the place as you read _The Amplified Bible_'s version of John 1:14 and the New International Version of Isaiah 40:5:

And the Word (Christ) became flesh (human, incarnate) and tabernacled (fixed His tent of flesh, lived awhile) among us; and we [actually] saw His glory (His honor, His majesty), such glory as an only begotten son receives from his father, full of grace (favor, loving-kindness) and truth.

—John 1:14 (AMP)

"And the glory of the LORD will be revealed, and all mankind together will see it. For the mouth of the LORD has spoken."

—Isaiah 40:5

DAY 3

*t*he Word who was with God in the beginning (John 1:1), Jesus Christ, lived on earth for 33 years. He left His unspeakably glorious and rightful heavenly home and His majestic royal robes to live in an unstable, man-made shack and in a body of flesh, vulnerable to sickness and even death.

Why would Jesus do that? See John 4:34.

_____

_____

When I talk with others who do not live as nomadic a life as we who are in the military, I am frequently asked, "Why do you do it?" While patriotism and love of my country and my husband are important, these do not top the list of my reasons.

To most, a career is a matter of choice. To a few, a career is a calling. A person who apart from God chooses a vocation is *driven*. One who is called is *drawn*. The former is driven by selfish ambition, propelled by a desire for honor, position, or prosperity, nudged on by mere necessity.

In contrast, the person who is called is drawn by a still, yet unmistakable presence, summoned by the voice of the Shepherd. "The watchman opens the gate for him, and the sheep listen to his voice. He calls his own sheep by name and leads them out. When he has brought out all his own, he goes on ahead of them, and his sheep follow him because they know his voice" (John 10:3–4).

God calls each of His children individually, personally, "by name"; however, He will not raise His voice above the clatter of a cluttered mind and heart. His call is spoken in a whisper, audible only to the hearts of those whose souls lie still before Him.

On the night before He was crucified, Jesus said something that should shape the way we look at our ever-changing lives and locales. Read John 17:18, and write out what He said.

_____

_____

Jesus shouldn't have to repeat Himself; but I'm glad He did. (At times, it takes me awhile to catch on.) **Read John 20:19–21, and write what Jesus said in verse 21.**

_____

_____

On what day did He say this? See also John 20:1.

_____

Jesus understands our transience. Being on the move was our Messiah's way of life. **What do you think Jesus meant in Matthew 8:20?**

_____

_____

_____

When Jesus set out to complete the work His Father had sent Him to do, where did He eat and lodge?

Luke 4:38

_____

Luke 7:36

_____

Luke 10:38

_____

Luke 5:29 and Matthew 9:10

_____

What instructions did Jesus give to His disciples as He sent them out?

Matthew 10:1–16

_____

_____

_____

_____

_____

_____

_____

_____

_____

_____

_____

_____

_____

_____

Luke 10:1–16

_____

_____

_____

_____

_____

_____

_____

_____

_____

_____

_____

_____

We won't have to wait a lifetime to reap the good fruit of following God and living out His will for our lives. I know this because of a recorded conversation between Peter and Jesus.

Peter said to him, "We have left everything to follow you!"

"I tell you the truth," Jesus replied, "no one who has left home or brothers or sisters or mother or father or children or fields for me and the gospel will fail to receive a hundred times as much in this present age (homes, brothers, sisters, mothers, children and fields—and with them, persecutions) and in the age to come, eternal life. But many who are first will be last, and the last first."

—Mark 10:28–31

God told Abram, "Do not be afraid, Abram. I am your shield, your very great reward" (Genesis 15:1). God gives not only His best to those who follow Him, He gives Himself. Who could ask for more?

DAY 4

My Heart, God's Address

*t*he night Jesus was arrested, He clearly told His disciples beforehand what they were about to face. Becoming sad and troubled, they realized He would soon be leaving them. Jesus then gave them (and us) a promise. **Read John 14:1–27.**

What did Jesus say He would ask the Father (v. 16)?

_____

_____

_____

_____

What are two other names for the Counselor who the Father would send (vv. 16–17, 26)?

_____

Who does not see or know Him (v. 17)?

_____

_____

Where does the Spirit of truth live (v. 17)?

_____

_____

Who "will come to [us]" and whom will we "see" according to Jesus's words in verses 18–19?

_____

Where is Jesus today (vv. 2, 3, and 20)?

_____

_____

Where are you (v. 20)?

_____

Where is Christ (v. 20)?

_____

_____

Who "comes to" those who love Jesus and obey His teaching (v. 23)?

_____

Note the use of "we" in verse 23. The *we* Jesus speaks of here is not new. Genesis 1:26 records another time God used a plural pronoun to refer to Himself. The original Hebrew word for *God* is a plural noun, *Elohim*.

What does *Elohim* make with us? See John 14:23 again.

_____

Jesus answered, "If a person [really] loves Me, he will keep My word [obey My teaching]; and My Father will love him, and We will come to him and make Our home (abode, special dwelling place) with him."
                                            —John 14:23 (AMP)

Abode: Greek, *mone*. From *meno*, meaning to remain, dwell. A mansion, habitation, abode. *Synonym: katoiketerion*. A place where one dwells *permanently*.

What have Christians been given? Read Colossians 2:9–10.

_____

What lives in bodily form in Christ?

_____

What did John see coming down out of heaven? Read Revelation 21:1–5.

_____

The "loud voice from the throne" calls this by another name. What is it? _____

Where will God dwell? _____

When will this happen? Read Revelation 22:7, 12, 20.

_____

Do you know that heaven is already a part of you? Luke 17:20–21 states, "For behold, the kingdom of God is within you [in your hearts] and among you [surrounding you]" (AMP).

In week 3, we studied the difference between sinful and sinless anger. We spent considerable time discussing and exploring Jesus's righteous rampage through the temple courts. **Turn to John's version of that day (2:12–22), and read what happened next.**

What did the Jews demand of Jesus (v. 18)?

_____

_____

Why did they demand it (v. 18)?

_____

_____

Write Jesus's answer (v.19).

_____

_____

_____

How long had it taken them to build this third temple (v. 20)?

_____

In contrast to the temple building, of what temple was Jesus speaking? _____

What is God's temple today?

1 Corinthians 3:16 _____

1 Corinthians 6:19 _____

2 Corinthians 6:16 _____

Jesus said that He is away preparing a place for us in His Father's house and that He promises to return and to take us there where He lives (John 14:1–3). Praise God! Until the day our mail starts arriving in crystal post boxes on streets of gold, God has chosen to make us—*our* hearts—*His* permanent address!

DAY 5

God's Heart, My Address

Like a bird that strays from its nest
is a man who strays from his home.
—Proverbs 27:8

One of Jesus's best-known parables is the story of a man who chose to leave his home. No one sent him away. No one asked him to leave. He simply had luggage tags that read "Anywhere But Here." (Oh, you've got some just like his? Me, too.)

The story of the lost son (or prodigal son, as some would refer to him) may be a familiar one to you, but read it again

anyway to refresh your memory and to feed your heart. Read Luke 15:11–31.

The man equates "home" with a certain person. Who is "home" to him (vv. 17–20)?

_____

_____

_____

What is the father's reaction when he sees his son "still a long way off" but headed toward home (vv. 20 and 22–24)?

_____

_____

_____

_____

_____

Every single person who's ever lived has willfully wandered from the Father's side. As Jesus was telling this story, He was essentially inviting us all back home. He was telling us, "Look! The porch light is on!"

The Father is watching and waiting, filled with compassion for you. He has His running shoes laced up and is prepared to burst out of the starting blocks the instant He sees you rounding the bend.

> *Softly and tenderly, Jesus is calling,*
> *Calling for you and for me;*
> *See, on the portals He's waiting and watching,*
> *Watching for you and for me.*

Come home, come home,
Ye who are weary, come home;
Earnestly, tenderly, Jesus is calling,
Calling, O sinner, come home.
                    —*Softly and Tenderly*
                    by Will L. Thompson

When asked where I am from, I have caught myself hesitating lately. Do they mean from where am I originally or from where did I just travel? With a father who served as a surgeon in the US Air Force and a husband in the US Navy, for me home base boundaries have become blurred. God knew an eternity ago our need for roots. He also knew how mobile people would become in the end times; therefore, I believe, He inspired the psalmist to write, "Your statutes are my heritage forever; they are the joy of my heart" (Psalm 119:111). God tells me that in His Word, I have a heritage that will last. "Heaven and earth will pass away, but my words will never pass away" (Matthew 24:35). In His Word, I have a permanent earthly address, a place where my mind and spirit reside in peace and safety. My body may sleep in lodging around the world, but my soul is continually at home in His Word.

I used to have a quote taped to my alarm clock that read, "The only permanent thing in this life is change." I believe there are two exceptions to this: God and His Word. No matter how many miles I travel, how many addresses I accumulate, how many churches I serve in, how many friends come and go, I have one immovable Rock in my life: God. "I the LORD do not change" (Malachi 3:6). I have a song in my heart because, "Your decrees are the theme of my song wherever I lodge" (Psalm 119:54).

My house number, street name, and zip code change regularly, and so do those of my friends. My address book's scribbles, eraser skid marks, and Wite-Out scabs attest to their impermanence. There is only one Friend from whom we will never receive a change-of-address card. His name is Jesus.

God wants us to experience permanence amid change. He has given us His Word. He has given us Himself.

Welcome home.

The Sacrifice of Separation

Robed in white ribbon and pink roses, the sanctuary sat shadowed and silent. Tiny golden flames of slender candles, tiered and tall, cast a warm, flickering glow across the altar where we stood. The voice of our pastor, gentle but firm, led us through our vows, phrase by phrase—his lead, then my echo, his lead, then Mark's echo. I stood face to face with the love of my life, my manicured hands in his, as guests, groomsmen, and bridesmaids listened in halted quiet.

"Marshéle, in taking the man you hold by the right hand to be your lawful and wedded husband, you must, before God and these present, promise to love and cherish him in that relation, and leaving all others, cleave only unto him, and be to him in all things a true and faithful wife so long as you both shall live. Do you so promise?"

My eyes never left Mark's, but to my right in my peripheral vision, I could see my parents giving their full attention to my promise from the front pew. To my left, my best girlfriends grinned in tearful delight. Behind Mark, his tuxedoed brothers and cousins stood tall and on shined tiptoe to hear my "I do."

I did, but did not fully know the height, depth, and breadth of my promise. Leaving all others and cleaving only to handsome him sounded sweet and honeymoonish and did not nor could not yet hint of the sacrifices ahead. That "I do" carried with it the full impact of a lifetime of saying good-bye over and over and living very far from those I love. The very witnesses to my vow to leave and cleave were part of my promise, the part I'd have to leave behind.

During the first months of matrimony, that leaving and cleaving stuff suited me just fine. Our first home, a one-bedroom, one-bath cozy love nest, was a perfect, snug fit for us two giddy newlyweds. The 320 miles of Sonoran Desert that separated Phoenix and San Diego were a wedge of distance we welcomed…at first.

As life unfolded and our Fort Fantasy became Fort Reality, that same desert, and later oceans, yawned far and wide and kept family and friends out of reach. Get-togethers with family and old friends, once instant, spontaneous, and free, now required schedules, air fares, and long weeks of waiting, followed by still more good-byes. Back home, life proceeded without us. Weddings took place. Nieces, nephews, and godchildren were born. Our parents faced health scares, surgeries, and terminal illness. Our grandparents died.

My father was diagnosed with amyotrophic lateral sclerosis (ALS), a killer more commonly known as Lou Gehrig's disease, and died 17 months later. Motor neurons are inexplicably attacked and murdered, strangling and canceling any neurological nourishment of the muscles. Thus, muscle tissue starves of any impulse, degenerates and shrinks, eventually leaving the victim fully paralyzed.

Because my husband's naval career wedged thousands of miles between my father and me, I was stricken with a different paralysis. The distance left me helpless to be the assistance to my mother and the encouragement to my father I could have been. My hands would have served him and my arms could have steadied him, but they could not reach him. My words could have uplifted him but were drowned in the ocean of mileage between us. My eyes

Hope for the Home Front Bible Study

could have watched over him, but the distance dimmed my vision. My ears could have listened patiently and intently to his heart's cry, but the chasm between us rendered his cry inaudible to me.

I searched for ways to unveil my heart, liberate my chained emotions, put words to my suppressed thoughts, and express my love for Daddy while he remained alive. Delta Airlines and AT&T buffered the pain of our separation at times. The visits developed into snapshots to be memorialized in a photo album. Phone conversations ended and dissolved into dial tones. I was left with only my prayers and faith in my God. Prayer was the one eternal link that bridged the ravine between my father and me. When I lifted my earthly father up to my heavenly Father, the bridge of faith carried me safely over the torrents of grief, frustration, and seeming injustice with which I struggled.

Prayer was the one eternal link that bridged the ravine between my father and me.

I was 2,500 miles from his bedside when he left this life. Long distance phone service was the conduit of our final conversation, an awkward monologue between a mourning daughter and her morphined, mute father.

The needs of the Navy not only kept us from our loved ones, but kept our loved ones from us in those times when we really needed a hand. We endured illnesses and surgeries and experienced births and babies many times outside the framework of family and friends and far from the familiar.

These scares and frustrations have taught both of us the importance of cherishing and redeeming the limited time we've been able to share with our loved ones in Mark's years of service. Mark and I agree that his military career is presently God's call on his life. His job promises no fame; US Navy SEALs are unsung heroes. It holds no potential for wealth; the defense budget is usually on the chopping block. Mark's choice to defend the United States, her ideology, and her people was and still is his obedient response to God's directive. For this reason, I rely on God and His Word during painful bouts with separation from those I love.

★ DAY 1

 can still see my daughter Jordan at two years young, galloping through the house toward the ever-ringing telephone. Her chubby little legs could propel her short and nimble self to the phone before anyone else. All I'd see was the blur of her bobbing blonde ponytail going beneath my elbow.

"I get it! I get it! I get it!" she'd squeal, hoping the call was for her. Twelve years later, besides the curls and the chubby little legs, not much has changed at our house. Jordan, now a slim, beautiful teenager, is still the first one to get to the phone. "I got it!" she hollers down the hall, positive the call is for her.

Today, thanks to technology, I'm not in a rush like Jordan to get to that ring. Answering machines, voice mail, and caller ID allow me to receive and return calls at my convenience and at a place and time that fit my needs. I like it that way. If we were stuck back in the days of curlicue telephone cords that anchored us to the kitchen wall, involuntarily glued to the receiver with a nosy neighbor, I'd be doubly the basket case I already am.

Hope for the Home Front Bible Study

We all get countless calls every day. Some we let the answering machine handle. Others are urgent and impossible to ignore. One day the "phone rang" for Abram. The caller ID read *God*.

Read Genesis 12:1–3 and eavesdrop on what God said to him.

The NIV Bible states in Genesis 12:1, "The LORD *had said* to Abram." Apparently this was *not* the first time God had placed a call to Abram.

When did God first call Abram? Read Acts 7:2–3.

_____

Where was Abram when he first heard from God?

_____

By the time we learn about this call in Genesis 12, where is Abram? Back up a bit and read Genesis 11:31 to find out.

_____

God promised to do seven things for Abram. What were they? Refer again to Genesis 12:2–3.

_____

_____

_____

_____

_____

_____

What did Abram have to do *first* before God would follow through on His promises? See Genesis 12:1.

_____

_____

What and whom did God tell Abram to leave?

_____

_____

_____

Where did God tell Abram to go?

_____

Have you ever sensed God's prompting deep within your heart of hearts to go and to do something outside of your comfort zone? What was it?

_____

_____

_____

_____

Why was it uncomfortable or difficult to do?

_____

_____

_____

Did your obedience mean leaving someone or something special behind? What or who was it?

_____

_____

_____

Hope for the Home Front Bible Study

What was Abram's response?

Genesis 12:4–5

_____

_____

Hebrews 11:8–10

_____

_____

Fill in the following blanks according to Hebrews 11:8:

> *By _____ Abraham, when called to go to a place*
> *he would later receive as an inheritance, _____*
> *and _____, even though he did not know where*
> *he was going.*
>
> —**Hebrews 11:8**

Read Romans 4:20–21. Abraham was commended for his response to God's call. Why?

_____

_____

DAY 2 ★

At the outset of His earthly ministry, Jesus chose 12 men to be His front-row students. He enrolled them in the By-His-Side Seminary, where for three action-packed years, He would teach, train, and prepare them.

Read Mark 3:13–19. Whom did Jesus appoint?

_____

_____

_____

Why did He appoint these twelve (v. 14)?

_____

_____

What were Jesus's three purposes in selecting these men (vv. 14–15)?

_____

_____

_____

Let's see how it happened for some of them. Read Matthew 4:18–22.

What were Simon and Andrew doing when Jesus called them (v. 18)?

_____

Write out Jesus's invitation to them in verse 19.

_____

What was their response (v. 20)?

_____

What were James and John doing the moment Jesus called them (v. 21)?

_____

Hope for the Home Front Bible Study

What was their response (v. 22)?

_____

_____

What and whom did they leave behind (v. 22)?

_____

Abram left country and kin to obey God's call. The first disciples left their livelihood and loved ones to follow Christ's lead. Paul the apostle left behind a pretty impressive resumé after a life-changing Damascus incident. He had been on the Jewish fast track.

What did he have going for him as far as the world was concerned? Read Philippians 3:4–6.

_____

_____

_____

God had an entirely different job for him to do, a different purpose for Paul's life. **Read Acts 9:1–19.**

What was God's call on Paul's life (v. 15)?

_____

_____

_____

What was Paul's response to God's plan? Read Philippians 3:7–14.

_____

_____

_____

In this passage of Scripture, we see the bottom-line reason why, ultimately, we leave all that is familiar to obey His call, and that is *to know Christ!*

Even our Messiah was appointed and sent by God from glory to Galilee. What was God's call on His Son's life?

Luke 19:10

_____

_____

John 17:22

_____

_____

John 17:26

_____

_____

What did Christ leave behind and/or give up to obey God's call? Read Philippians 2:6–8.

_____

_____

Do you sense a calling on your life? What do you feel personally invited by God to do?

_____

_____

_____

_____

_____

I believe with all my heart that God called me to be Mark's wife and the mother of his children. God weaved the call He had on Mark's life (to be a godly warrior) together with the call He had on my life (to be a godly wife and mom). Yes, I left behind those I love and hold dear to follow my man around the globe, but I can truthfully echo Paul:

> *But whatever was to my profit [family, friends, higher education, career, comfort zone] I now consider loss for the sake of Christ.... I want to know Christ and the power of his resurrection and the fellowship of sharing in his sufferings [being rootless, away from family, hearth, and home].... I press on to take hold of that for which Christ Jesus took hold of me.... Forgetting what is behind and straining toward what is ahead, I press on toward the goal to win the prize for which God has called me heavenward in Christ Jesus.*
>
> —Philippians 3:7–14

Whether you are a Mesopotamian on the move, a minister, a mom, or a military wife, you are created and called by God to do a particular, wonderful something *only you* are uniquely designed to do. And when God calls your number, I hope you'll leap and lunge through the house squealing, "I get it! I get it! I get it!"

> *For he chose us in him before the creation of the world to be holy and blameless in his sight.... In him we were also chosen, having been predestined according to the plan of him who works out everything in conformity with the purpose of his will.*
>
> —Ephesians 1:4, 11

DAY 3

*W*e are asked to do a lot of things. Requests for our help and time seem endless. From the PTA to the booster club to fund-raising groups to the church nursery to the needs of our neighbors, everyone seems to be asking us to help. How many times has the phone been for us and we've weaseled out of it by placating the person with feigned politeness and a put off: "May I call you back a little later?" or "May I get back to you on that?"

Learning when and how to say a polite but convincing no to all the puppy-eyed pleas is an ongoing challenge. Knowing when to say yes requires an equal measure of discernment. The ability to do either without hesitation, without second-guessing, without remorse is a skill Jesus clearly had and demonstrated. It is a skill that He aims for us, His disciples, to master. Because He knew and obeyed the voice of His Father, He walked through His earthly days with clarity and purpose, never hesitating or straying from the path marked out for Him. He calls us to the same—a life guided by divinely set priorities regardless of discomfort, difficulty, cost, or sacrifice.

In my book *Hope for the Home Front*, I began my acknowledgments with "Thank you, Mark, for always believing in me, loving me, and encouraging me to never give up. I'd marry you again and follow you to the moon."

Well, we could have been to the moon, tagged it, and returned by now if we added up all the mileage we've covered together to date, yet I don't regret one inch of it. From my starry-eyed "I do" to my clear-eyed "I'd marry you again," I've weathered Navy life well for one reason alone: I knew that He who called me was at the helm, designing and directing my discipleship journey.

Answering the call and making the commitment to ministry, to marriage, or to any kind of life on the move is never without cost. When Jesus called others to follow Him, some, as we've already studied, immediately left all to do so, but not everyone was sold on the Savior. Some answered the Messiah's call with a first-century version of our 21st-century "May I call you back later?"

I tell you, now is the time of God's favor,
now is the day of salvation.
—2 Corinthians 6:2

As they walked with Jesus along the road toward Jerusalem, three different men in six short verses teach us much about the cost of following Jesus.

Read Luke 9:57–62. What did the first man promise Jesus (v. 57)?

_____

His words remind me of a promise made more than a thousand years before by a woman also on a road that lead toward Jerusalem. Her name was Ruth. The promise she made to her destitute mother-in-law, Naomi, meant an uncertain and difficult future awaited her, yet this did not scare her away.

Read Ruth 1:16–17. Write her promise here.

_____
_____
_____
_____
_____

Getting back to the passage in Luke 9, read Jesus's response to the eager disciple (v. 58). What do you think Jesus wanted this man to understand?

_____

_____

_____

_____

The holes of foxes and the high-rise houses of fowls highlight with stark contrast the handing over of hearth and home that those who answer God's call must make.

How did the second man answer Christ's call to follow Him (v. 59)?

_____

_____

If *physically* dead people cannot bury other physically dead people, what do you think Jesus meant when He said, "Let the *dead* bury their own dead." (Hint: There is a difference between being physically dead and being spiritually dead.)

_____

_____

_____

Instead of hanging around town, what did Jesus want this man to do?

_____

_____

In your daily routine, how are you personally proclaiming, declaring, preaching, demonstrating the kingdom of God...

...to your children?

_____

_____

...to your extended family members?

_____

_____

...to your co-workers?

_____

_____

...to your neighbors?

_____

_____

Read Luke 9:61–62. What did the third man want to do before he would follow Jesus?

_____

_____

_____

I don't believe Jesus meant that we should neglect our family relationships. I do believe that Jesus was underscoring how absolutely focused on Christ we must be as we follow Him. The man pledged his loyalty to Christ, but first wanted to "go back." Do you recall the fate of Lot's wife who merely "looked back"? Hmmmm.

Complete Jesus's response to this man (v. 62).

_____ _____ *who puts his hand to the plow and*
_____ _____ *is fit for* _____ *in*
the kingdom of God.

—Luke 9:62

What do you think Jesus was telling these three would-be followers that he or she should be willing and prepared to do without?

The first man—Luke 9:57–58

_____

_____

The second man—Luke 9:59–60

_____

_____

The third man—Luke 9:61–62

_____

_____

Read about a fourth wannabe witness in Luke 18:18–23. Even with his tedious attention to obey God's commandments, what one thing, according to Jesus, did this man still lack?

_____

_____

_____

_____

_____

This man's treasure remained earthbound. What was the perfect prescription that would free this man to fully follow Christ?

_____

_____

What was this man's reaction to Christ's remedy?

_____

_____

What was he unwilling to do without?

_____

_____

Doing without the comforts of a permanent home, the stability and structure of extended family, the security of an expected inheritance, and the power of earthly wealth were roadblocks for these disqualified disciples. Worldliness says, "Me first." Godliness says, "His kingdom first." What do you say?

> _"But seek first his kingdom and his righteousness, and all these things will be given to you as well."_
> —Matthew 6:33

DAY 4

i was a feisty 15-year-old. I knew everything. I knew much more than my parents and didn't need or want anyone to tell me how to live my life. I remember one particular afternoon when my teenage tongue bought me more than I'd bargained for. My mother and I constituted too many women under one roof. Most of our mother/daughter discussions dissolved into tears and arguments in those days.

Her firm resolve to train me up in the way I should go rammed head-on into my rebellious ways. Her colors were nailed to the mast. She had no plans of surrendering to my persistence. I can't remember what lit my fuse that day, but I do recall my reaction. She had told me no to something I desperately wanted to do. She wouldn't budge. End of discussion. She turned her back to me and proceeded to prepare dinner. The tempest in my head found its way to my tongue and I seethed, "I hate you," enunciating every consonant.

She didn't even turn around to respond to me. She didn't need to. Unbeknownst to me, my dad had arrived home from work earlier than unusual. He had heard the whole thing. All I saw was the blur of the backside of my father's hand sailing around the corner toward my head. Thwonk! My father's medical school ring sank into my forehead like David's smooth stone in Goliath's skull. "Don't you ever talk to your mother like that again, young lady!" my typically soft-spoken and patient father reprimanded. Shocked by his presence, startled by the blow, and embarrassed by my own behavior, I stumbled backward a few steps, holding my hand over my throbbing brow. "You will love your mother. Don't ever use that word *hate* like that again," he finished. It was a lesson in respect and honor that I never forgot. Perhaps the bluish mirror-image impression of *University of North Carolina 1966* that remained between my eyes for several days had something to do with that. The indention and the soreness lessened, but the lesson I learned that day did not: Hate will have no welcome mat on the doorstep of my family relationships.

That's one big reason Luke 14:25–26 threw me for a loop! Read that passage. What did Jesus say to the large crowds who were following Him? Write verse 26 here exactly the way He said it.

_____

_____

_____

_____

_____

This seeming contradiction to all I've been taught causes me to rub my furrowed brow as I remember Dad's reprimand. *Hate my family?*

Read the portion of Scripture that precedes this warning (Luke 14:15–24), so you will have context for studying selected words from Luke 14:25–26 and their original Greek meanings.

Come: *érchomai.* When used with the preposition *opíso*, this word means to follow, to become the follower or disciple of anyone.

Hate: *miséo.* To love less.

Life: *psuchés.* From the root *psúcho*, meaning to breathe. *Psuchés* means the vital breath, the life element through which the body lives and feels, the principle of life manifested in the breath, one's soul.

Disciple: *mathetés.* From *manthános*, which means to learn or understand. *Mathetés* is one who accepts the instruction given to him and makes it his rule of conduct.

Spiros Zodhiates, PhD, or Dr. Z as I refer to him, explains this word *hate* in this position and context so well: "In Luke 14:26 Jesus contrasts love to family with love to Himself.... Here Jesus asserts His deity. Every member of man's family is a human being, and the love shown to humans compared with the love shown to Jesus Christ, God in the flesh, must be so different that the former seems like hatred.... When it comes to loving God, however, He is placed in a unique position" (*The Complete Word Study New Testament*, 1991).

Refer back to the word studies in this session. Write your own amplified version of Luke 14:26 by substituting the selected words with your paraphrased understanding of each word's original definition.

_____

_____

_____

_____

_____

_____

_____

Read Matthew 10:37. This verse uses *miséo*, too, and helps us to better understand Luke's use of *hate*.

What excuses did those who had been invited to the great banquet (in Luke 14) give to the host?

Verse 18

_____

_____

Verse 19

_____

_____

Verse 20

_____

_____

Read once more your expanded version of Luke 14:26.

Has the Lord called you to go somewhere, to speak to a certain person or group, to do something for Him, to give up something or someone to follow and to know Him, to come alongside Him as His fellow worker? What invitation from God keeps coming to your mind as you work through this week's study?

_____

_____

_____

Have you come up with reasons why you can't or won't accept His invitation? What are _your_ excuses for not obeying His call?

_____

_____

_____

What or who stands in your path as you "seek first his kingdom and his righteousness"?

_____

_____

Remember, Jesus Himself knows what it is to leave the familiar. He not only left heaven to live with us, but had to leave His earthly hometown in order to do all of God's will. He said, "Only in his hometown and in his own house is a prophet without honor" (Matthew 13:57).

Why, when we know Jesus promised in Matthew 6:33 that "all these things will be given to you as well," do we hesitate to leave our familiar comfort zone to follow Him? There is no rewind button on the VCR of life. Opportunities and invitations from God to serve God and to get to know Him in all His greatness come in big, sure, unmistakable moments of clarity. The presence and prodding and power of the Holy Spirit perfectly deliver the divine proposition.

If proximity to family and the familiar is your excuse for not accepting God's call on your life, I encourage you with all my heart to prayerfully reconsider your RSVP. Serving God, living out His plan, seeing Him work His purposes in and through you, witnessing His faithfulness to provide for you every step of the way, and above all, knowing Him intimately are the magnificent adventure you and I don't want to miss.

DAY 5

*t*he sun was just peeking over the eastern foothills and beginning to stream into the kitchen of the farmer's wife. The barnyard animals, drawn by the aroma of percolating coffee, peered into her kitchen window to watch her prepare breakfast: eggs and bacon. The horse leaned over to the sheep and asked, "Do you know the difference between the chicken and the pig right now?"

"Naaa-aaa-aaa," the sheep bleated. "Whaa-aaa-aat is the difference between the chicken and the pig at breakfast time?"

The horse replied, "One made a contribution. The other made a commitment."

Jesus calls us not to make just a contribution, but to make a wholehearted commitment to following Him wherever and whenever He leads. He tells us, "If anyone would come after me, he must deny himself and take up his cross daily and follow me. For whoever wants to save his life will lose it, but whoever loses his life for me will save it. What good is it for a man to gain the whole world, and yet lose or forfeit his very self?" (Luke 9:23–25).

We must be willing to leave everyone and everything dear to us for a little while or for a lifetime if obedience to His will demands it. Jesus said, "any of you who does not give up everything he has cannot be my disciple" (Luke 14:33).

What or whom have you given up in your life as you have followed Jesus and committed to do God's will for your life?

_____

_____

_____

_____

List the six people, places, or things you love the most in the entire world:

_____

_____

_____

_____

_____

_____

Is there a familiar place or a special someone you still play tug-of-war with God for? What or whom have you not yet been willing to give up so you can love Him foremost and serve Him completely?

_____

_____

_____

_____

Which do you think you've made more often—a contribution (cluck, cluck) or a commitment (oink)? _____

Jesus wants us to arrive at the point where we can honestly say that our love for Him is so great, so intense, so transcendent, so boundless that, in contrast, it makes our love for others look like loathing. He wants us to prayerfully pilgrimage to the place where our love for Him is a raging, all-consuming fire that shrinks our love for others to a mere glowing ember.

We are to love our neighbor as we love ourselves, but Jesus _never_ told us to love _Him_ like we love one another. Our regard for the royal Son of God should make our love for any son of man look like repulsion. Of course we are to love one another! Jesus commanded us on the night He was arrested, "Love each other as I have loved you" (John 15:12). Our love for family, friends, and even strangers is to match the love Christ had for us on the cross. In extreme contrast, our love for Jesus Christ should make that kind of sacrificial, brotherly love look like enmity for everyone and everything else, including the ones most precious to us.

After writing your name in the first blank that follows, write the names of your dearest ones in the other blanks:

If [insert your name here] _____
comes to me and does not hate (love less)
_____ and _____ ,
_____ and _____ ,
_____ and _____
—yes, even [her] own life—[she] cannot be my
disciple.

—Paraphrased from Luke 14:26

Seeking God's will always involves saying good-bye. I believe "God works for the good of those who love him, who have been called according to his purpose" (Romans 8:28). Because I love Him and am called to be by my husband's side and absent from my dear ones, I believe all the trials caused by our separation are intended to crown me and conform me to His likeness, not to destroy me.

The comfort in it all is that Jesus knows exactly how I feel. He left His Father in heaven to answer God's call on His life. From the instant of holy conception in Mary's womb until He surrendered His spirit on Calvary, Jesus enjoyed only one face-to-face visit with His "family," the Father and the Holy Spirit, on the day of His baptism in the Jordan River. For 33 years, He worked, persevered, loved, obeyed, and endured all of God's will for His life. Surely He understands the longing of wanting to go home! Yet He left everything to do God's will, including the One He loved most. I am comforted to know He will never require me to endure anything He hasn't already experienced.

Read Matthew 12:48–50. Whom does Jesus consider to be His family?

_____

_____

Read Luke 18:29–30. What did Jesus promise to those who leave all for the sake of God's kingdom?

_____

_____

_____

***When* will he or she receive this?**

_____

_____

Do you recognize anyone in your life as a sister, a mother, or a grandmother whom God has given to you because you are so far away from your own?

_____

_____

I encourage you to stop and write a note to that person now, just as you did in week 1 to your "Joshua" or "Caleb," to let her know that you consider her a fulfillment of Luke 18:29–30 in your life.

To those who obediently and humbly and wholly respond to God's call with an Isaiah-style "Here am I, [Lord]. Send me!" (Isaiah 6:8), God promises a glory that outweighs all suffering. We are to keep our eyes fixed not on what is seen (our family, our friends, our career, our money), but on what is unseen (the kingdom of God and our unique part in it). "For what is seen is temporary, but what is unseen is eternal" (2 Corinthians 4:18).

> *Don't put it in my ear, but in my hand.*
> —Russian Proverb

God is perfectly capable of caring for the loved ones we must leave behind. Put them in His hands and believe in your heart that "he is able to guard what I have entrusted to him for that day" (2 Timothy 1:12).

What's So Good About Good-bye?

It is good, when faced with a separation, that we realize more deeply than ever before how much that special someone means to us.

It is good that we stop our frenzy of activity to express our appreciation for the comfort, the friendship, the support, the laughter, the tears, and the encouragement the person has added to our journey.

It is good to be reminded that life is brief, at best, with no dress rehearsals, and the seasons we are privileged to share together are even more fleeting.

Good-bye is good if it teaches us to cherish life and breath, strength and sound mind, and the moments we are allowed to walk side by side with a friend.

Good-bye is good if, in that difficult moment, we stand still long enough to give thanks to God for the lessons we've learned together, the love given, and the love received, recognizing that these blessings are gifts from the hand of God.

Good-bye is good if, as a result of the relationship, both people are stronger in the faith, better equipped, more confident, and more fervently motivated to serve the Lord using the spiritual gifts entrusted to us.

Rank: A Right Perspective

anging pictures is the grand finale after the orchestration of unpacking in a new home. When the portraits, prints, and antique photographs are on the walls of our new home, then I know we have finally arrived. As we wrapped up one PCS, two contrasting portraits grabbed my attention. An engrossing comparison interrupted my progress.

I sat Indian-style on the floor and propped the two photos of my husband side by side on my lap. On my left was a ruddy, mustached sailor uniformed in his dark blue crackerjacks. His chest and arm were decorated with the red and black insignia, stripes, and ribbons of a salty second class petty officer. On my right was a striking, clean-shaven man clad in choker whites and adorned with black shoulder boards, gold stars, and the emblems of an ensign. The contrast of one man in two uniforms triggered a flashback to Mark's commissioning day at Officer Candidate School (OCS).

After seven years of service as an enlisted sailor and four months of OCS, Mark, a second class petty officer, was to be instantly transformed into a fresh ensign. He left one world and crossed the threshold into another while marching to the tune of "Anchors Aweigh." Amidst the fanfare and celebration which spanned 48 hours, I quietly studied my mutating husband as he floated through each ceremony, donned in his new wardrobe, eager in his new role. After much contemplation, I concluded that I was still married to the same man. The changes Mark had undergone were only superficial. His new insignia were pinned to his lapel, not to his character. Rank reclassified him, but his core person remained unscathed, intact, and unchanged.

The portraits slid and settled crooked in my lap, splicing the mental film that was reeling through my memory. I blinked away the trance and resumed my comparison of the two photographs. The transitional years between the enlisted and the officer photos had added a few crow's-feet beside my husband's eyes and had plucked a few hairs from his receding hairline—minor, insignificant changes in relation to the dramatic, complete makeover I somehow expected.

I put the enlisted portrait aside and admired the photo of Mark in his choker whites. I remembered the day Mark received his commission and I visited PSD to get a new identification card. In the past, clerks in the same office had acknowledged me with a "Yeah, what do ya need?" As the young man glanced at the papers I handed him, I witnessed borderline rudeness become gentlemanly gallantry. The typewritten "Ensign" switched his gears and caused his treatment of me to radically change. "What do ya need?" cleaned up to "How may I help you?" "Yep" improved to "Yes, ma'am." "Nope" became a polished "No, ma'am, I'm sorry." With Mark's promotion came two wonderful niceties: the words "please" and "thank you."

The inequities of rank have teetered my concept of justice. In the anticipation of being frocked an officer's wife, I somehow believed the indignity I experienced as an enlisted wife would give way to a clear understanding of and new respect for the military system. I supposed the new vantage point would give me a clear view of its virtue and sense.

I was mistaken. My new perspective only deepened my convictions. The rules and regulations that accompanied rank were often taken too far. The ligaments intended to strengthen the body of defense were pulled dangerously tight past the point of due respect and would snap, injuring those standing in its ricochet. A system designed to produce unity and orderliness, I learned from experience, could be taken past its limits, causing disunity and injurious separations between folks.

Despite my disillusionment, I now recognize the need for rank. I agree it plays a vital role in the security of our nation. The system, with its official grades and levels, is purposely designed to create and promote order for the task of defending and preserving certain freedoms. In combat situations, there must be no question as to who gives orders and who obeys them. Confusion would incite panic. Anarchy always ends in defeat.

 # DAY 1

C an you imagine a business without a boss? A classroom without a teacher? A church without a pastor? A city without a mayor? An airport without air traffic control? A state without a governor? A military without a commander in chief? A nation without a president? A world without national leaders? The universe without God? *Anarchy. Chaos. Futility.*

A home, classroom, workplace, city, state, nation, or world without established headship is as senseless, disfigured, and useless as a headless body. Life in a leaderless world would be a flustered mess on the best of days. Havoc and mayhem would be the norm. Life at one end of the spectrum would be an aimless wandering any and every which way. On the other end of the spectrum, life would be a complex, tangled knot of lawlessness and war.

Cluttered confusion benefits no one. God knew this before time began. What does 1 Corinthians 14:33 teach us about God?

_____

_____

God, by His very nature, is orderly. His name is *Yahweh Shalom*, the Lord is Peace (Judges 6:24). Artwork always reflects the heart of the artist. It makes sense then that an orderly God would create the heavens, the earth, and everything in them to be orderly.

Read Genesis 1:2. How is the earth described in the beginning?

_____

_____

Genesis 1:1 through 2:2 is the account of the creation. Read through this and notice that as God *created* all things He also *organized* His creation. Then as He structured creation, He gave responsibility and rule to some. As you read the verses below, find and record words and phrases that express His acts of organizing, placement, and structuring. I've done the first one for you as an example.

Genesis 1:4
As God created light, He *separated* the light from the darkness. Separating is an act of organization.

Genesis 1:6–7

_____

_____

Genesis 1:9

_____

_____

Genesis 1:12

_____

_____

Genesis 1:14–15 (Watch for the first mention of responsibility and rule here.)

_____

_____

_____

Genesis 1:16–17

_____

_____

_____

Genesis 1:21

_____

_____

_____

Genesis 1:25

_____

_____

Separation. Gathering. Marking of seasons, days, and years. Organization. Classification of plants, fish, birds, and land animals. "And God saw that it was good" (Genesis 1:12, 18, 21, 25).

Read Genesis 1:26–28. What responsibility did God originally give to mankind?

_____

_____

_____

_____

_____

Subdue. Rule. Govern. Order. Peace. God gave order to His creation. He separated and gathered. He organized and classified. He delegated rule and entrusted governance.

Through Eve and then Adam, sin entered the world and caused chaos, havoc, and ultimately death for mankind. Later, God sent the great flood to silence the disorderly din. In His mercy, though, He safely and neatly tucked Noah, Noah's family, and a careful categorization of animals inside a timber boat that had been painstakingly constructed to fit God's specifications.

After the flood, what did God promise Noah concerning the structure and rhythm of life? Read Genesis 8:22.

_____

_____

_____

What did God do that would ensure man's rule over the animals? Read Genesis 9:2.

_____

_____

Seasons. Sequence. Continuity. Rhythm. Routine. Submission. Respect. Rightful rule. Peace. God is the ultimate organizer.

ot only has God created order and ordained rule for the big picture, but He has also determined who is in charge of all created things, from vast nations to our individual families and homes.

What do you learn about God's reign and plan for mankind's orderliness in the following verses? Note whom God appointed to lead whom.

GOVERNMENT IN THE HEAVENLY REALM: THE FATHER

Psalm 9:7

_____

_____

_____

_____

Psalm 47:7–8

_____

_____

_____

_____

Psalm 95:3–5

_____

_____

_____

_____

Government in the Heavenly Realm: The Son

Psalm 110:1

_____

_____

_____

_____

_____

Hebrews 1:3, 13

_____

_____

_____

_____

_____

Colossians 1:18

_____

_____

_____

_____

_____

Ephesians 1:22

_____

_____

_____

_____

_____

Government in the Heavenly Realm:
The Holy Spirit

Joel 2:28

_____

_____

_____

_____

_____

Luke 11:13

_____

_____

_____

_____

_____

John 1:33

_____

_____

_____

_____

_____

1 Corinthians 6:19

_____

_____

_____

_____

_____

GOVERNMENT ON THE EARTH

Romans 13:1–7

_____

_____

_____

GOVERNMENT IN THE HOME

Ephesians 5:21–24

_____

_____

_____

1 Corinthians 11:3

_____

_____

_____

Ephesians 6:1–4

_____

_____

_____

Each of us has been entrusted with a level of responsibility and authority. What has God given you authority over in His order of things?

_____

_____

_____

What Scriptures can you base this on?

_____

_____

_____

_____

I realize that your study time yesterday and today were a bit longer than usual. I applaud you! You did great to hang in there! It was important that we invest this time in learning about God's intended order for His creation. This knowledge serves as a foundation. It is a valuable review that supports our study of a right perspective of authority for the remainder of our week's assignments.

★ DAY 3

 e know that God's plan for order in heaven and on earth is flawless. "As for God, his way is perfect; the word of the LORD is flawless" (Psalm 18:30). Although we may disagree with those appointed to lead us, His method of management is always for our good and for His glory. God's ordained leaders in heaven, on earth, and in the home are gifts to us so "that we may live peaceful and quiet lives in all godliness and holiness" (1 Timothy 2:2).

But what about Hitler? Stalin? Pol Pot and the Khmer Rouge? Hussein? What about unreasonable bosses? What about unrealistic, insensitive husbands? Sadly, because we are human and we "all have sinned and fall short of the glory of God" (Romans 3:23), the ones appointed to lead us don't always do the right thing—no one does right 100% of the time. God's way is perfect; man's isn't.

Way back in Eden, Satan reached out and grabbed God's plan for earthly order with his grimy hands and left his greasy fingerprints all over the divine design. We still see those same smudges today. Daily we read and hear about every type of misuse of authority at all levels of government, from systematic genocide and racial or religious persecution ordered by countries' highest offices to domestic abuse and violence in our own homes, husbands against wives, parents against children. Every single case is evidence of Satan's perversion of power, a distortion of God's perfect system of order.

What current event or trend that is clearly a perversion of power comes to your mind?

_____

_____

_____

_____

_____

Does/did this take place on an international, national, or local level?

_____

Based on your understanding of the trend or the event, what is/was the root cause of the abuse? What grimy "fingerprints" did Satan use to seed this sin?

_____

_____

_____

_____

Consider the following characteristics and activities, and determine for each whether it is more likely a tendency for those who have been *given* authority or a blunder for those *under* authority. Place a check mark under the appropriate heading.

	TRAPS FOR THOSE *GIVEN* AUTHORITY	TRAPS FOR THOSE *UNDER* AUTHORITY
Boasting		
Complaining		
Covetousness		
Cruelty		
Disobedience		
Disrespect		
Greed		
Haughtiness		
Injustice		
Jealousy		
Love of power		
Lust for power		
Mutiny		
Pride		
Pulling rank		
Rebellion		
Self-centeredness		
Throwing one's weight around		
Unteachableness		
Unwillingness to serve		

Hope for the Home Front Bible Study

Do some of these sins trip up *both* the leaders and those being led? Which ones?

_____

_____

_____

_____

The View from the Top: Traps for Those Given Authority

Today we will study just a few of the traps into which people entrusted with positions of leadership and power might fall. Rather than simply telling you what they are, I want you to discover them for yourself from the true biblical accounts. I want you to see for yourself the choices and actions of real people who struggled with this gift of authority.

Read each Scripture portion. Let the Holy Spirit be your magnifying lens as you look for Satan's fingerprints on God's gift of order. Identify the sin of the one in charge.

Read 1 Kings 12:25–33. Who was in charge? What was his sin?

_____

_____

_____

_____

Read John 11:45–48. Who was in charge? What was the sin?

_____

_____

_____

_____

Read Daniel 4. Answer the following questions.

Who was in charge (v. 4)?

_____

What did he dream (vv. 10–18)?

_____

_____

_____

_____

_____

Whom did the tree represent (v. 22)?

_____

What was the sin of the one in charge (v. 30)?

_____

_____

_____

What was the consequence of his sin (vv. 31–32)?

_____

_____

_____

What was the lesson God wanted the king to learn once and for all (vv. 32–37)?

_____

_____

_____

Do not exalt yourself in the king's presence, and
do not claim a place among great men; it is better
for him to say to you, "Come up here," than for
him to humiliate you before a nobleman.

—Proverbs 25:6–7

Jeroboam loved his power and the praises of the people so much that he ignored and outright disobeyed God's commands in order to preserve his high position. The Jewish leaders' plot to murder the Messiah was based on their fear of losing their rank and honor among the people. Babylon's king, Nebuchadnezzar, lauded himself and lost his mind.

Pride, lust for power, and boasting top the list of the many pitfalls into which those in charge can slip. Other traps for those at the top include unkindness, injustice, unwillingness to serve others, an unteachable heart, greed, and selfishness.

Those of us with children and a home are entrusted with the authority and the skill to manage them. We who are employed outside the home are responsible to lead employees and manage resources. Our husbands serve as leaders in our communities as foremen, chairmen, pastors, officers, commanders, master chiefs, master sergeants, majors, captains, colonels, admirals, and generals. Every one of us faces temptations to pull rank and throw our weight around, misusing the gift of leadership, authority, and trust. Each of us is tempted to love our position more than the ones we lead.

Each of us has felt like boasting and have struggled with conceit at times. Each of us has to make a deliberate decision, a conscious choice to remain teachable, to humbly serve those under our charge and to constantly remember that "the Most High is sovereign over the kingdoms of men and gives them to anyone he wishes and sets over them the lowliest of men" (Daniel 4:17).

DAY 4

*i*n God's order of things, there are the leaders and the led, the governors and the governed, those who give orders and those who obey them. My husband served seven years as an enlisted sailor. Four of those seven, I was married to him. I was, as they called me, an enlisted wife. Our rank meant that our view of life in those early years of marriage was from the bottom looking upward. When we weren't bowing our wills in submission to the chiefs and the COs in charge, we were craning our necks to see what life was like for "the other half."

The View from Below:
Traps for Those Under Authority

In those days, I was unaware of the traps Satan sets uniquely for those who should follow and do the bidding of the ones in charge. Instead of finding fullness and satisfaction in our blessed but humble status, I found myself craving the other half's seeming financial ease and overall better quality of life. My curiosity gave way to coveting. My discouragement dissolved into disrespect. Instead of respecting those with rank, I resented them.

We have a son and two daughters. God sent all three of them to the Waddell household within less than six years. Keeping my little flock together on any errand or outing was like herding cats. I often found myself counting heads—at times quietly, other times out loud—one, two, three…one, two, three…one, two, three…to make sure there was a full muster at all times. I guess all that mini-census-taking stuck. Today we affectionately refer to Joshua, Jordan, and Jenna as J1, J2, and J3.

Hope for the Home Front Bible Study

The Lord told Moses twice to count His kids. The Old Testament Book of Numbers gets its English name from all the counting of kids, the children of Israel, that takes place in chapters 1 and 26. *Numbers*, however, is not the title its author, Moses, gave the book. The Hebrew title is *Bemidbar*, which means "in the desert." I think Moses might respond with a chuckle and a nod of his head to the newer title found in our Bibles. He would likely agree that the book is a record of the many *number* of times God's kids complained and rebelled on their long trip *in the desert!*

They complained about *everything* from the man in charge to the menu. Despite all their gripes, God remained gracious; yet our perfect Father wasn't about to let His kids be whiners, so for every whimper, whine, and murmur, there was a delay. Their wonderful promised destination remained just out of reach as long as they bellyached.

Miriam and Aaron, Moses's older sister and brother, are perfect examples. They represent us, the led and the governed, who bristle and balk at the one God has named to be the boss.

Read Numbers 12. On what topic did their conversation begin (v. 1)?

_____

On what note did it end (v. 2)?

_____

_____

How did the Lord respond (vv. 4–10)?

_____

_____

Gossip and griping led to grabbing for Moses's God-given gavel. The Lord heard their entire conversation and called them to the tabernacle for an immediate trial. No jury was necessary. The Judge Himself had heard every word. Not only that, God heard the silent hatred simmering in their hearts toward the order and authority He had designed and assigned. The Lord reprimanded Aaron and Miriam and left. Miriam was leprous. All three had learned a lesson.

What did Aaron call this gossip, griping, and power grab (v. 11)? _____

God in His mercy, and at the request of Moses, mended Miriam, but this sin among the siblings wasn't without consequences. Miriam, the one who instigated the insurrection, was disciplined, and once again God's people were delayed. Once again, the Promised Land was postponed.

Does this happen in our lives today? Do you think our dreams are delayed or God's promises to us are ever postponed when we grumble against the ones God has given authority?_____

Bad-mouthing the boss can blossom into a bad disease. Too much tongue wagging ends in tragedy. Just ask Miriam. I don't know about you, but I'd rather keep my mouth shut and keep heaven's doors open wide. I'd rather keep my heart free of grumbling so my hands can be filled with dreams come true.

Do you feel like disrespectfully spouting off? Before you do, please consult the boys who mocked Elisha and met a fate worse than that of Goldilocks (2 Kings 2:23–24).

Are you grappling with greediness for more than God has given you? Go ask Gehazi about it first (2 Kings 4 and 5). Ask him if getting what he wanted was worth the consequences.

Are you turning green with jealousy over the promotion God gave to someone other than you? Ask Joseph's brothers what it felt like to give in to their jealous thoughts about Joseph (Genesis 37).

Do you suffer with a case of sticky-fingered selfishness? Ask Lot how much Sodom and Gomorrah were worth in the end (Genesis 13 and 19).

Jealousy, hatred, division, selfishness: this is the pattern of the flesh (Galatians 5:19–20), that is, until the *Word* became flesh. He lived with us, teaching us by parable and by perfect example how to both humbly lead and humbly serve.

Tomorrow, we will look to Jesus, to His commands and His example of what it means to be a humble servant and an effective leader.

DAY 5

*t*hey say that character is caught, not taught. We understand all too well the old adage, "Do as I say, not as I do." We know the ongoing struggle and humbling truth that we don't always walk the talk, and we don't always practice what we preach.

Jesus did. We know from Scripture that while Jesus commanded us to love, value, and serve one another without partiality, He could confidently say, "Do as I say *and* as I do." He truly did practice all He preached. He talked the walk and walked the talk. He not only taught us how to treat one another, He demonstrated to the fullest extent what obedience to His commands looks like.

Today we will start by studying the commands and teachings of Jesus concerning how we are to treat each other. We will then explore how He exemplified all He requires of us.

Begin your study time by reading each portion of Scripture that follows. As you read, listen to your Savior's heart. Glean from each of His parables one crystallized, bottom-line instruction as it relates to this subject of *serving one another*. Put this main idea into your own words. Write it in the space provided.

Matthew 18:23–34

_____

_____

_____

Luke 10:25–37

_____

_____

_____

Luke 11:5–8

_____

_____

_____

Luke 14:7–11

_____

_____

_____

Luke 14:12–14

_____

_____

_____

⋆ **Jesus was teachable.** Luke tells us that when Jesus was only 12 years old, His parents searched for Him for three days after unintentionally leaving Him in Jerusalem after the Passover celebrations. **Read Luke 2:41–51. What was Jesus doing when Mary and Joseph finally found Him (v. 46)?**

_____

_____

_____

Jesus knew well the proverb, "He who walks with the wise grows wise" (Proverbs 13:20) and "let the wise listen and add to their learning, and let the discerning get guidance" (Proverbs 1:5). As an adult, Jesus remained teachable, consulting the One in authority over Him, the heavenly Father.

How did Jesus, in word or by His actions, demonstrate a teachable heart in the following verses?

John 5:19

_____

_____

Matthew 26:39

_____

_____

Matthew 26:42

_____

_____

Jesus was teachable. As a boy He listened to the experienced and the wise. As an adult He asked His Father for direction. **In what ways are you still learning, still growing?**

_____

_____

_____

_____

In what areas are you still unreachable and unteachable?

_____

_____

_____

_____

★ *Jesus was respectful.* Jesus knew He was God's only begotten Son, yet while He lived on our earth, He respectfully submitted Himself to those in earthly authority. **To what authorities did Jesus show respect?**

Luke 20:20–26

_____

_____

Matthew 17:24–27

_____

_____

Jesus respected those to whom God had given authority. He understood that those leaders had been put in place to maintain God's intended order and to fulfill His purposes. **Do you understand this? Do you struggle with this? If yes, how?**

_____

_____

_____

⭐ *Jesus showed no partiality.* I love this about Jesus! He wasn't too proud to sit and chat with the rejects of society. Neither was He too self-denigrating to strike up a conversation with VIPs. While He knew His own worth, He also recognized the worth of every soul around Him.

Jesus associated with people of every background, status, and rank. Other folks' social standing meant nothing to the Savior. He didn't concern Himself with a person's outward appearance; He saw the person's heart (1 Samuel 16:7). He interacted with people from across the social spectrum of His day.

Who were some of these people Jesus interacted with and what was the social standing of each?

Matthew 4:18

_____

_____

_____

Matthew 4:24

_____

_____

Matthew 8:2–3

_____

_____

Matthew 8:5–7

_____

_____

Matthew 9:9–10

_____

_____

Matthew 19:13–15

_____

_____

Luke 7:36–50

_____

_____

John 3:1–2

_____

_____

Do you interact with a wide variety of people or do you spend most of your time only with those who look and sound like you?

_____

_____

_____

Why?

_____

_____

_____

_____

Ask God to bring someone to your mind and to your path today who looks different, dresses differently, talks differently, or believes differently than you. Ask Him how He wants to bless that special one through you. **Write the person's name here and what you plan to do to bless them.**

_____

_____

_____

Jesus gave us many other leadership and servanthood examples. He demonstrated perfect, God-pleasing exercise of authority as well as God-honoring surrender, submission, and obedience in the proper order of all things.

His ultimate demonstration of obedience to the Father's will happened at Calvary, when on a Roman cross He gave up absolutely everything for us. "He humbled himself and became obedient to death—even death on a cross!" As a result, "God exalted him to the highest place" (Philippians 2:8–9).

In view of God's design of authority, rank, and order, what attitude does God want us to maintain? Read Philippians 2:5.

_____

_____

_____

Humble yourselves, therefore, under God's mighty hand,
that he may lift you up in due time.

—1 Peter 5:6

A right perspective of rank is critical to preserving the good in the system, as well as to controlling its tendency to spill into areas it does not belong. ***Rank must not be allowed to play the slightest role in the way we value and treat other people.*** Stars and stripes sewn to a sleeve don't increase the value of any human soul. Likewise, the absence of such insignia does not communicate one has any less worth. A seaman recruit and his wife deserve just as much kindness and respect as the fleet admiral and his wife. A private and his wife merit as much courtesy as a sergeant major and his. The airman and his family are as worthy of a polite response as the general's. Each deserves loving acceptance and respect simply and profoundly because each is loved by God and is created in His image.

One morning as Mark dressed for the day, I sensed his anxiety. He was to be the ringmaster of a dog and pony show for several captains and admirals scheduled to arrive that day. I put my arms around his neck, looked deep into his green eyes, and said, "Remember, Honey, the admiral puts his pants on one leg at a time, just like you." Mark chuckled and relaxed.

All ranks of personnel, from E-1 to O-10, share the same heart, mission, and vision for our nation. The only difference is in the duties assigned to each person. Rank and responsibilities differ; their souls, significance, and sacrifices don't. The cliché "You can't take it with you" is trite but right. Once an admiral, general, master chief, or sergeant major retires from military service, he or she can no longer command the same respect from the civilian world that he or she once did in the military realm. Sooner or later the reality hits that respect is earned, not assigned. Just as the black shoulder boards, gold stars, red stripes, colorful ribbons, and lustrous medallions will one day be placed and stored in a shadowbox, our bodies and worldly achievement will be laid in a larger box and given back to the dust. In the end, all that matters is our treatment of God and His highest creation, people. Friends and family are the only things that will survive past the grave. A glimpse of eternity can do much to correct an impaired view of people.

> *He has showed you, O man, what is good. And what does the* Lord *require of you? To act justly and to love mercy and to walk humbly with your God.*
> —Micah 6:8

Foreigners Focused on Forever

*A*merican soldiers and sailors live and work on every habitable continent on our planet, stationed in at least 148 countries and in five US territories. From Albania to the United Kingdom, from Armenia to Uzbekistan, from Australia to Vietnam, from Afghanistan to Yemen, from Angola to Zimbabwe, and from Antigua to Venezuela, nearly 20 percent of US Armed Forces are protecting Americans and American interests abroad. While a quarter of a billion folks back home are enjoying mega malls, pro sports, prime-time TV, first-run movies, smooth highways, and manicured backyards, these men and women and their families live as foreigners around the globe for the sake of freedom.

As the majority of Americans happily munch lunch at a million McDonald's, a minority of us who can't hurry on down to Hardee's must brave questionable noodle stands in East Asia, browse labyrinths of crowded fruit and vegetable markets in South America, and belly up to kebab stands in the Middle East for falafel and hummus in a pita. America's motorists mumble about gas prices and rush hour while one fifth of her military must share the road with darting rickshaws in the Far East, bicycles in Bangkok, rams and ewes in Romania, bull camels in Bahrain, and lorries in London that drive in the left lane! With addresses at new latitudes and longitudes, these service members and their families must change the time on their wristwatches, the wardrobes in their closets, and the words in their mouths to match that of their host country, adapting not only their appliances but their attitudes as well.

Being paleface *haolis* in Hawaii's Polynesian, *shaka-brah*, *poi*-pounding culture at the beginning of Mark's naval career was only a tiny taste of the adventures that we would experience as a family later when, thanks to BUPERS, we became *gringos* in Panama and *auslanders* in Germany. Orders like these to overseas assignments not only required a passport, a series of vaccinations, and tedious, probing overseas screenings, but also came with the guarantee that the experience would alter our lives and perspectives permanently. Moving *across* the country was one thing. Relocating to a *different* country was a whole new ball game...an away game, that is, from the first pitch to the last run, with a completely different set of rules, referees from another league, and millions of fans rooting for the home team, *not* ours.

Our three overseas assignments stuffed into one decade taught me many lessons. I learned how to speak three more languages, how to make Wiener schnitzel and German potato salad, and how to drive safely (translated "fast!") on the autobahn. I learned how to barter with Kuna Indians, how to broil bass caught from Gatún Lake, how to drive safely through city riots, and how to fry plantains in Panama. I learned how to crack open a coconut, how to hula dance, and how to make leis with plumeria blossoms in Hawaii. I learned how to unravel the webs of European mass transit systems and how to dodge overloaded, lopsided banana trucks, sloths, and anteaters at night on unlit Central American roads.

I learned that I own way too much and so many others don't own enough. I learned to be thankful for the blessings I have.

I learned that my homeland's headlines on CNN International sound a lot different when I'm on the outside looking in. I learned that the whole world doesn't love America or Americans the way I do. Some folks are still angry about events that happened generations ago. Some don't want to learn English because of the bad taste we left in their mouths. I learned there are many people, though, who are grateful to America, those whom America helped, fed, and liberated. I learned to relax and not to take life or myself too seriously. I learned there's a lot of fun out there for those willing to chance it.

Most importantly, I learned that our experiences as Americans living in a foreign country drew striking parallels *to the challenges Christians face as believers living in an unbelieving world*—parallels worthy of our time and exploration.

From this fountainhead of realization, streams of application trickled down, watered every plain of my being, and brought new life to my sphere of influence. I identified the lessons I had learned from living as a foreigner in a foreign country and then began to apply them, to put them into action on a *faith level* regardless of my physical address.

 ## DAY 1

*W*hen we lived overseas, we rightfully retained our American citizenship. We didn't mutate into Panamanians in Panama or into Germans in Germany; rather, we valued our birthright as American citizens and kept careful tabs on the whereabouts of our priceless passports.

Hope for the Home Front Bible Study

We were advised to blend in with the locals, to dress in culturally appropriate clothing, to use English softly and sparingly in public places, and not to blazon our American pride in ways that would be considered grossly arrogant. For the sake of safety, we modified our mannerisms, shifted our schedules, and selected our outfits to respect their customs. We did not, however, stop being Americans. Our birthright and core loyalties never changed.

Citizenship: A Choice, a Privilege, and a Trust

Six billion folks people our planet. About 280 million of them are Americans. Less than five percent of the world's population is made up of citizens of the United States of America. If you were a customs agent at any overseas airport, you would have to stamp 95 foreign passports before meeting your first American.

Most Americans today are US citizens by birth. Many others immigrated to this country and became citizens through a lengthy and tedious process. Simply *wanting* to be a US citizen is not enough. There are specific requirements, forms, and procedures an applicant must follow and fulfill.

There are three types of residents in this or any other country: citizens, aliens, and visitors. To prepare yourself for this week's study, consider the definitions of each as found in the third edition of *The American Heritage Dictionary*.

Citizen: "A person owing loyalty to and entitled by birth or naturalization to the protection of a state or nation."

Alien: "1. An unnaturalized foreign resident of a country. 2. A person from a very different group or place, owing political allegiance to another country. 3. An outsider."

Visitor: "One who goes or comes to see for reasons of business, duty, or pleasure."

Unlike the alien and the visitor, a person with US citizenship enjoys certain privileges and protections:

- A US citizen has the privilege of participating in the US government on the local, state, and national levels.
- A US citizen is entitled to carry a US passport.
- A US citizen can utilize and enjoy services of all US embassies and consulates. He or she comes under the protection of the US when away from the homeland.
- A US citizen is entitled to bring members of his or her immediate family into the US as permanent "green card" residents.
- A US citizen has immunity from deportation.

Hang in there with me! I realize this is beginning to sound a lot like a high school civics class; but I believe God will richly bless you through His Word as He reveals and we discover what *He* has to say about this topic of *citizenship*.

What is your citizenship? (USA, UK, etc.)

_____

How did you become a citizen of your country? Check one.
- ❑ **By birth in my country**
- ❑ **By birth outside my homeland to parents with citizenship**
- ❑ **As a child when my parents became citizens**
- ❑ **By naturalization**

Hope for the Home Front Bible Study

This week we will study this subject of citizenship and apply what we learn to deepening our walk with Christ. **Read the Scripture "passports" listed below and identify each person's legal citizenship.**

Abraham—Genesis 11:27–28; Acts 7:2

_____

Rahab—Joshua 2:1

_____

Ruth—Ruth 1:1–4

_____

Esther—Esther 2:5–7

_____

Jesus—Luke 2:4–7
  Where was Jesus born? _____
  Where did He grow up? _____

Peter—Mark 1:21, 29

_____

Paul—Acts 21:39; Acts 22:3 (See chapter 21 for context.)
  Where was Paul born? _____
  In what city was he brought up? _____

What a melting pot of nationalities and cultural backgrounds the family of God is!

*W*hen you first meet someone, what are some of the questions you generally ask in your first conversation? **List some of those questions below.**

_____

_____

_____

_____

The first question that came to my mind was, "So where are you from?" The other person's answer to this one question gives us gobs of information and context for continuing and guiding our conversation.

When asked where *you* are from, what do you say?

_____

What context, information, reactions, and even stereotypes do you think pop into your listener's mind when she hears where you are from?

_____

_____

_____

It's so easy to jump to conclusions about another person when we prematurely categorize her based solely on her home of record. Remember Nathanael's first reaction when He heard Jesus was from Nazareth? "Nazareth! Can anything good come from there?" (John 1:46). Like Abraham, many of us for many reasons move from place to place. Like Rahab, some of us were "rescued" from our doomed status quo and plunged into a new place and people group. Like Esther, some of us grew up in adoptive or foster homes far from our original home. Like Peter, Paul, and even Jesus, some of us have left our home to obey the plan and the will of God.

So where are you from *really*? Where in reality is your citizenship? Earth's residents are citizens of 193 independent nations. Many of these countries allow dual citizenship. The math becomes mind-boggling when one calculates the possible combinations of countries. The probabilities send the numbers off the charts. The statistics increase the choices and flavors of citizenship exponentially.

As far as God is concerned, there are only *two* possible passports: one with the world's stamp of approval and one with heaven's seal. All human beings who have ever lived and breathed on this planet are ultimately citizens of one or the other. No dual citizenship is permitted by either "country."

Where is the citizenship of believers and followers of Jesus Christ? Read Philippians 3:20.

_____

How does Peter describe this celestial citizenship? Read 1 Peter 2:9–10.

_____

_____

How does knowing your citizenship is in heaven make you feel?

_____

_____

How does it affect your perspective on life?

_____

_____

★ # DAY 3

_M_ost of us are citizens of our country simply because we were born there. Our birth within our nation's borders meant all the afforded privileges, blessings, and protections were ours, instantly, from our first, startled, bare-bottomed wail. Many people falsely believe that being born in a "Christian" country, in a nation founded on faith in God's Word, makes them automatically a Christian.

What did Jesus say about citizenship in heaven? Read John 3:5–8.

_____

_____

Have you been birthed only physically (in the flesh)?

_____

Have you been "born again," that is, birthed _spiritually_?

_____

_____

God wants all people to be born again, that is, born by His Spirit into His eternal family, and to be given all the rights, privileges, and protections promised to those who are His own.

How is God described in 1 Timothy 2:3–4?

_____

_____

_____

Read Romans 10:9–13 to see how a person is born into God's kingdom.

To be saved and become a citizen of heaven, what must we do with our mouths (v. 9)?

_____

To be saved and become a citizen of heaven, what must we do in our hearts (v. 9)?

_____

_____

What is the result of believing (v. 10)?

_____

What is the result of verbally confessing our belief (v. 10)?

_____

What happens to the nations' borders for those who are now saved (v. 12)?

_____

_____

Why (v. 12–13)?

_____

_____

In contrast, Satan wants no one to be saved or born again. His aim is...

   ...to close and secure all borders around his "nation" of the unsaved,

   ...to deceive his "residents" into believing they can never leave their darkness,

   ...to lie to his "countrymen" and convince any seekers that citizenship in God's kingdom is undesirable or unattainable,

   ...and to squelch anyone's plans to emigrate.

God wants to give everyone a relationship with Himself and citizenship in His kingdom, not condemnation. His borders, like His arms, are standing wide open for any who will come to Him through faith in Jesus, His Son, the Christ.

Jesus has done *everything* necessary to secure our citizenship in heaven:

✷ He gave His life to purchase our passport to Glory.

✷ He bled and died to pay the price for our safe passage.

✷ He rose from the dead to guarantee our permanent place with Him throughout all ages to come, life never ending!

✷ He even promised to personally escort us on our pilgrimage.

Squatter or Citizen?

If you are not certain you have citizenship in heaven, you can pray in all sincerity this prayer or one like it and be assured of your permanent residence in the heavenly realm.

Father, I know that I am a sinner. I confess my sin to You and turn from it now. I believe Jesus is Your Son and that He died on a cross to pay for my sins against You. Please forgive me of my sins. Give me new birth into

Your family. Make my life new and clean. I give You control of my life. I surrender my will to Yours today. Thank You that my citizenship is in heaven now where You are. Thank You that You now live in me. Help me to live for You until I am home with You. Amen.

When prayed from a sincere heart, becoming a citizen of heaven is that simple! The applications, exams, and procedures for citizenship into any other country are tangled in red tape. The process of becoming a citizen of heaven is instant and permanent because it is written with the priceless red blood of Jesus Christ.

Praise be to the God and Father of our Lord Jesus Christ! In his great mercy he has given us new birth into a living hope through the resurrection of Jesus Christ from the dead, and into an inheritance that can never perish, spoil or fade—kept in heaven for you, who through faith are shielded by God's power until the coming of the salvation that is ready to be revealed in the last time.

—1 Peter 1:3–5

DAY 4

*O*kay, so I'm a citizen of heaven, *you say. So what? How does that affect my life here and now? What good does my passport to paradise do me today? How is my life as a citizen of heaven any different from that of unbelieving Joe Schmoe next door?*

This is so exciting to me! Look back to day 1 of this week's study, where we overviewed the difference between a citizen, an alien, and a visitor. I included a list of the basic rights, privileges, and protections of a US citizen. I want you to discover how these basic citizenship rights parallel and apply *scripturally* to your life as a believer in Jesus Christ and a citizen of heaven.

✶ *A US citizen has the privilege of participating in the US government on the local, state, and national levels.*

The basic role of government is to provide protection from enemies and the intervention necessary for peaceful community and national life. Just as earthly nations have enemies, the kingdom of God has enemies.

In what area of your life are you struggling today?

_____

_____

_____

With whom or with what are you wrestling?

_____

_____

_____

With what, *according to God's Word*, are you actually struggling? Read Ephesians 6:12.

_____

_____

_____

Where are these enemies of yours?

_____

_____

When God raised Christ from the dead, what place of honor did He give to His Son? Read Ephesians 1:20.

_____

_____

What is Jesus seated *above*? Read Ephesians 1:21.

_____

_____

_____

What are *under* Christ's feet? Read Ephesians 1:22.

_____

Don't miss this! As a believer in Jesus Christ, God made you alive and saved you by His grace. What did He do next? Read Ephesians 2:6.

_____

_____

Since you are seated with Christ in the heavenly realms, what, according to Ephesians 1:22, is under *your* feet?

_____

In your present struggle, please remember that our God has given heavenly citizenship to you who are in Christ. That means that you are seated with your Savior. Whatever you struggle with is under the very soles of your feet! You have been graciously granted the privilege of participating in God's government at the highest level! There is nothing that is opposed to you in the heavenly realm that is not subject to the authority in Jesus's name, which you have been given as a citizen of heaven.

Along with that authority, we have been given something **more** for participating in God's government. What have we been given? Read 2 Corinthians 10:3–4.

_____

_____

✮ *A US citizen is entitled to carry a US passport.*

No paperwork is involved in gaining citizenship in heaven. "Man looks at the outward appearance, but the LORD looks at the heart" (1 Samuel 16:7). The Lord Most High looks for two things on the heart of the one seeking heavenly citizenship.

The first is found in Ephesians 2:13; Colossians 1:20; and 1 Peter 1:18–19. What is it?

_____

The other is found in 2 Corinthians 1:21–22; Ephesians 1:13–14; and Ephesians 4:30. What is it?

_____

_____

At this very moment, many people are attempting to cross our borders and enter our country using illegal passports and documents. Likewise, many souls attempt to enter heaven with insufficient proof of citizenship. As a citizen of heaven, your passport has been stamped by the bleeding, pierced palm of Jesus and sealed by the Spirit of God. These and only these validate your citizenship!

✮ *A US citizen can utilize and enjoy the services of all US embassies and consulates, coming under the protection of the homeland at all times.*

Hope for the Home Front Bible Study

When we lived in foreign countries, we always made sure we knew where the US embassy and consulate offices were located. Because we did not always live on the base, we had to know where to go in a crisis. We kept the telephone numbers, addresses, and maps to the American Embassy on hand wherever we lived or traveled. An embassy is a building that contains the offices of the ambassador to that country, houses his or her staff, and is considered sovereign soil. It is a place of security, refuge, asylum, and escape for all citizens of the country it represents. The sentries on duty there will shield and insulate the ones needing cover.

The church, the local body of believers in Jesus Christ, is the Christian's embassy in this world. We are to shield and shelter one another in crises and in times of heightened threat. We are to intercede with our home of record on behalf of those who need protection from the outside. We need to be a living, breathing place of comfort and security for all who seek freedom. We are to cushion one another from the crushing crowds and to be the harbor of safety for those who need cover from the storm. Once inside an embassy, a person is safe and considered off-limits to all those who angrily surround the building in pursuit of him. The same is true of those who are *in* Christ.

⋆ A US citizen is entitled to bring members of her immediate family into the US as permanent "green card" residents.

Living overseas with three children tripled our fun. It also taught me the importance of reminding them often of their homeland and where our loyalties are. Because our youngest had celebrated five of her nine birthdays on foreign soil, America, the land of her birth and citizenship, and its customs were vague memories to her at best. She frequently asked questions about the US, its glories, its struggles, and her loved ones who lived there. When it was finally time to return to the States, she understandably wrestled with fears of the unknown and the unfamiliar.

As Christians, we have the God-given responsibility to our children of passing on information about our heavenly home, such as Who lives there and exactly how to get there. We are entrusted with the stewardship of modeling our homeland's ways and customs for our children to learn and to imitate. We are also commanded to introduce them to our presiding governor, Jesus, so they can have personal knowledge of and lifelong rapport with Him. Then, when it's time for them to go home, they will wrestle with fewer fears of the unknown and the unfamiliar.

★ *A US citizen has immunity from deportation.*

This one is my favorite! Too many Christians fear losing their salvation. They live with the dread that in the end their citizenship in heaven will be revoked. They tremble inwardly with thoughts of being turned away at the gates.

There are several reasons Christians doubt the permanence of their place in heaven. These include sin, wrong teaching, an emphasis on feelings and emotions, lack of knowledge of God's Word, unbelief in God's Word, and plain and simple spiritual warfare. If you know any of these spiritual muscles are weak in your walk of faith, pursue and commit to an exercise plan! Dig into God's Word on the matter and don't quit digging until your treasure is in your hand. Seek godly counsel from mature and seasoned believers and learn from them.

The truth is that once you are redeemed, your name is written in the Lamb's book of life, which is heaven's roll call and citizenship roster, and will *never* be erased.

Jesus Himself promised this. Read Revelation 3:5 and write it here, word for word.

_____

_____

_____

_____

The name of every person who has ever placed his or her faith in God's finished work in Christ Jesus is written in permanent ink in heaven's registry, the Lamb's book of life. The ink flows blood red from His pen and makes your name ineradicable.

> *I write these things to you who believe in the name of the Son of God so that you may know that you have eternal life.*
>
> —1 John 5:13

DAY 5

*a*s I write today's homework, thoughts of next week's rapidly approaching Thanksgiving holiday interrupt my concentration. All the preparations are on my mind, from clearing my messy dining room table to making my grocery list to carving the turkey. God tapped me on the shoulder and reminded me to stay focused on finishing this week's study for you.

"If you must think about Thanksgiving," He said, "then ponder the Pilgrims." And in His own, unique, gentle, and gracious way, He continued to give me the message He has for you.

A pilgrim is defined as "a traveler...on a long journey...of exalted purpose...to a sacred place" (*The American Heritage Dictionary*, third edition).

Some of the first permanent English settlers in America in 1620 were called pilgrims. They had traveled from England on a long and dangerous journey for the "exalted purpose" of worshipping God freely in a "sacred place" called New England!

The writer of Hebrews describes all the heroes of our faith as "pilgrims on the earth" (Hebrews 11:13 KJV). Why are these people called "pilgrims on the earth"? Read Hebrews 11:13–16.

As citizens of heaven, we must always remember that this earth is not our home. We are pilgrims just passing through on our way to a "country of [our] own...a better country—a heavenly one."

Jacob was an old man by the time he was reunited with his son, Joseph, in Egypt. When Joseph introduced his dad to the Pharaoh, the king asked the old man his age. How did Jacob answer the Pharaoh? Read Genesis 47:9.

How many are the years of *your* pilgrimage today?

**For those of you who have a King James Bible, look up
1 Peter 2:11. How does Peter address *us*, his readers?**

_____

_____

_____

_____

The story is told of an elderly couple who was returning home to their native Great Britain after serving for decades as Christian missionaries in remote areas of India. Coincidentally, the couple cruised home aboard the same ship that carried the Queen of England. When they finally arrived at their destination, the couple watched as the queen was escorted off the ship in dramatic flare and pomp, welcomed by cheering crowds and stately bands. Confetti filled the air and the music crescendoed as the queen disembarked.

In contrast, no one was there to meet the elderly missionary couple. No one carried their heavy trunks and baggage. The band did not play one note to welcome them ashore. The man, now gray and shorter than when he had left to serve God abroad, turned to his wife and said, "After all these years of hardship, sickness, hard work, and sacrifice, you'd think that *we* would be the ones getting such a grand welcome."

The woman smiled, and with a twinkle in her clear blue eyes, answered her husband, "Honey, we're not home yet."

Jesus told a parable about a wheat field that was overrun with weeds. Jesus was giving us an illustration of the world in which we live. Believers and unbelievers grow up and live side by side…for now. Sometimes it's difficult to distinguish between the "wheat" and the "weeds." **Read Matthew 13:24–30.**

Is your life surrounded by "weeds"? Do you feel that your corner of the field is nothing but impostors, rebels, and mockers? Do you ever wonder *how in the world* you are supposed to live for the Lord in your corner of the world? Explain.

_____

_____

_____

The solution is to keep sending your roots deeply into the rich soil of the Savior's Word and wait patiently for the Lord to keep His promises. A harvest date has been set! In the meantime, remember that Jesus prayed for us who are "pilgrims on the earth."

Read John 17:14–17. Why does the world hate believers in Jesus (v. 14)?

_____

_____

_____

What was Jesus's prayer request in verse 15?

_____

"Sanctify them by the truth; your word is truth," Jesus prayed. The word *sanctify* means to set apart for sacred use or to make holy. What is it that sets us apart from the "weeds"?

_____

_____

_____

_____

I want to leave you with one more encouraging word. Excluding the hundreds of thousands of active duty US service members, more than three million US citizens live in foreign countries. One-fourth of them live in Canada, one-fourth live in Western Europe, and a tenth live in Mexico. The rest reside in 100 other lands. They are business professionals, teachers, spouses, ministers, missionaries, entrepreneurs, journalists, children, aid workers, federal employees, retirees, and students. All of them carry a US passport, retain US citizenship, and enjoy all the privileges and protections America promises to its own.

Similarly, our brothers and sisters in the Lord live in every country on the planet. They are business professionals, teachers, spouses, ministers, missionaries, entrepreneurs, journalists, children, aid workers, federal employees, retirees, and students. All of them are citizens of heaven through faith in God's one and only Son. All of them are sprinkled by His blood, sealed by His Spirit, and protected by His holy name.

One day we will all be together in His presence singing His praises in every language. We will emigrate from this world as we've known it and end our pilgrimage at His throne.

> *After this I looked and there before me was a great multitude that no one could count, from every nation, tribe, people and language, standing before the throne and in front of the Lamb.*
>
> —Revelation 7:9

The Language of Life

ark and I lingered, embracing in the frame of our front door, warmed by the rising California summer sun, still intoxicated by our fairy-tale wedding and whirlwind honeymoon. Mark's leave had come to an end. The thought of an eight-hour separation seemed intolerable to us. Starry-eyed, we whispered sweet nothings to each other one last time, then reluctantly pried ourselves apart. Mark drove away, blowing kisses to me in his rearview mirror. Proud of my sailor and giddy with love, I watched until he was out of sight.

I busied myself tidying our tiny apartment that morning in an effort to whisk away not only the dust but also the work day that separated us. As I cleared the kitchen counters, I came to a small heap of receipts, gum wrappers, pennies, and other pocket contents from the fatigues Mark had worn the day before. Curious, I stopped to read a small, crumpled note scribbled in my new husband's handwriting: "Burn marriage license."

Burn marriage license? Horrified, I pondered the possible explanations. Goose bumps raised every hair on my body. I shivered as the aftershocks rose up my legs and spine. Only three explanations held water: (1) Mark was a KGB secret agent planted in US Naval Special Warfare and needed a bona fide American wife for a cover, (2) he was an assassin about to make his hit, or (3) he had a girl in every port and he intended to keep it that way. For the remaining seven hours, I sobbed in confusion and searched our apartment for phone bugs, minicameras, and other tools of espionage.

When I heard Mark's '66 Mustang backfire as he parked at the curb, I gathered my composure and tried to greet him with a smile. One look at him and my façade was shattered as a new flood of tears burst forth. Instead of being greeted with a warm welcome, Mark was bombarded by a barrage of whos, whats, and whys—one senseless question and incomplete sentence after another.

The words I promised myself I would not utter came screaming out: "Why, tell me, why are you planning to burn our marriage license?"

Mark, shell-shocked but still intact, gently wrapped his strong arms around my tense, trembling body. He tenderly looked into my swollen, bloodshot eyes and, with a smirk on his lips, said, "Honey, that's just military talk. To burn something means to make a copy of it. I just needed to make a copy of our marriage license," obviously doing everything in his power to restrain the oncoming guffaw. Several seconds of silence followed. Shades of astonishment, disbelief, embarrassment, and then relief flushed and colored my face. We laughed away the last half hour of California sunset in each other's arms once again.

DAY 1

*a*fter training for a couple of decades, I now speak broken Militarese. Because my marriage to a military man did not come with a Militarese-to-English/English-to-Militarese pocket dictionary, I have spent much time and effort memorizing, pronouncing, and decoding this foreign language.

Likewise, having lived overseas several times, I've learned that making the effort to speak the country's language went a long way in making and building relationships with the people. Even though I made good comedienne material as I tried to roll my tongue and gurgle my throat like the locals, my wholehearted attempts won their respect and their loyalty most of the time—that is, except the time I exclaimed, *"Estoy embarazada!"* ("I'm pregnant!") to a Panamanian woman when I meant to say "I'm embarrassed!" You better believe I was! Another faux pas was the time I exclaimed, *"Ich bin kalt!"* for "I am cold." My German friend gently explained to me that the sentence structured that way meant I was sexually frigid. Oops.

Tongue twisters and word blunders happen every day. Most mistakes are small and insignificant. Some are unforgettable. **Share one of your own experiences in which your words or someone else's caused a significant misunderstanding, whether harmless, hilarious, or hurtful.**

_____

_____

_____

_____

_____

_____

These slipups of syntax and slang drive home a central truth for our study this week: as "strangers in this world," we need to know and speak "the language" of those around us. Usually that means shelving our "Christianese" and being willing to stay within a context that our unbelieving family, friends, and neighbors understand.

Hope for the Home Front Bible Study

Getting to the Root of Misunderstandings

When the last drop of the last puddle had evaporated into the blue sky above Mt. Ararat, there was a knock at Noah's door. **Who was it? Read Genesis 8:15.** _____

Noah and his family and the animals had been confined to the ark for one year and ten days! (And you thought summer vacation with the kids and the dog was long!) More than a year before, God had told Noah, "Go *into* the ark." **What did God tell Noah to do now? Read Genesis 8:16–17.**

_____

_____

Once the zoo had been dismissed, Noah built an altar to the Lord, the first altar mentioned in the Bible, and sacrificed burnt offerings on it. God made a promise to Noah. **What did God promise Noah? Read Genesis 8:21–22.**

_____

_____

_____

_____

Then God blessed Noah and his sons and gave them specific instructions. What three things did God command Noah and his sons to do? Read Genesis 9:1, 7.

_____

_____

What were the names of the three sons of Noah? Read Genesis 9:18–19.

_____

Fast-forward a few generations. Read Genesis 11:1–4 and answer the following questions.

Where had all the grandchildren of Ham, Shem, and Japheth settled (vv. 1–2)?

_____

How many languages did the people speak (v. 1)?

_____

What was their common goal (v. 4)?

_____

_____

Look back to Genesis 9:1, 7. How well had Noah's sons followed God's instructions?

Had they been fruitful? _____

Had they increased in number? _____

Had they filled the earth? _____

There on the plain of Shinar, which is in modern-day Iraq near the Tigris and Euphrates rivers, all mankind milled around together with one mission in mind: to disobey God's clear directive to fill the earth. This act of disobedience was simply the fruit of hearts steeped in pride and egotism. They wanted a "name for themselves," essentially wanting the reputation for being self-made men, rendering God unnecessary. They wanted to stay in Shinar and not fill the earth as God had commanded their three forefathers to do.

What happened as a result? Read Genesis 11:5–9.

_____

_____

_____

_____

_____

_____

Can't you picture it? Joe says, "Hey, Bob, pass me a hammer." All Bob gives Joe is a dumb stare. Bob, in his new tongue, replies, "Stop talking with your mouth full." Joe responds by dropping his jaw. A million scenes like this happened simultaneously across sunny Shinar and escalated into a frightful, frustrated panic. Thus, their God-defying project came to a screeching halt.

It is interesting to note that the city the rebels were building was called Babel. According to the NIV footnote for Genesis 11:9, the word *Babel* sounds much like the Hebrew word *balal*, which means "confused." The footnote goes on to say, "The word (Babel) is of Akkadian origin and means 'gateway to a god.' The Hebrew word used here (*balal*) sounds like *Babel*, the Hebrew word for Babylon and the origin of the English word *babel*."

The English word *babel* is defined as "a confusion of sounds or voices." To *babble* means "to utter meaningless words or sounds, to talk foolishly" (*The American Heritage Dictionary*, third edition).

We could conclude that many misunderstandings begin with the blunder of babbling, one person foolishly uttering meaningless words to another. The *root* of misunderstandings many times is a prideful, rebellious desire to do things our own way, not God's way. The *fruit* of misunderstandings then is wasted time, energy and resources, hurt feelings, a lot of needless confusion, or worse, the dishonor of God's name.

In your opinion, do people do more effective communicating or babbling? Why?

_____

_____

_____

It is not the Lord's will that we *be* confused or *cause* confusion. Simplicity, straightforwardness, and transparent clarity are communication skills that honor God and reflect His character to the world. It is my prayer that this week you will learn more fully how to effectively communicate your faith in Jesus Christ and the truth of God's Word to those whose lives are socked in by dark clouds of confusion.

> *For God is not a God of disorder but of peace.... But*
> *everything should be done in a fitting and orderly way.*
> —1 Corinthians 14:33, 40

★ DAY 2

 was born and raised in North Carolina. *I'm a Tar Heel born, Tar Heel bred, and when I die, I'm a Tar Heel dead* (always spoken singsong style to the UNC fight song). My mama says I was prayshus (precious), prob'ly 'cuz I's the spittin' image of my daddy.

Because my great grandparents came from yonder Statesville way, I's raised on fried livermush, grits, chopped BBQ, and Yoo-hoo chocolate milk drinks. I have fond memories of making biscuits (honey, cut that dough half in two), shelling butter peas, stewing okra with my grandmother, and sopping red-eye gravy with PawPaw. I can still picture PawPaw playing his harmonica so passionately that we'd all duck to miss the flying spit. And he shore could play them spoons! First thang he'd say to me as he came through the back door after work was "Gimme some sugar." After a sweet peck, he'd purse his lips and say, "You a bird." Then he'd sink into his favorite chair, pick up the Kannapolis Chronicle, and fall asleep 'cuz he was tard and plain give out. Those were the days when birds had wangs, cars had tars, and sinners were on their way to hale. We warshed our hands before suppa, said "yes, sir" when Daddy said "Git down from there," and played possum when he and Mama checked on us after bedtime.

It wasn't until we moved to Arizona when I was nine years old that I realized not everyone spoke "Y'all," that is, Dixie's dialect of English. When I said, "Hey!" (instead of hello), my new classmates snickered and sneered, "Hay is for horses!" Embarrassed, I quickly learned to say, "Hi, you guys!"

The pocketbook and billfold I once carried became a purse and a wallet. Women now wore nylons, not hose, and men wore slacks, not trousers, in the sophisticated southwest.

That surprise immersion on the playground into a "foreign" dialect during elementary school was the beginning of higher learning for me. It elevated my parlance and pronunciation to a whole new plane. It was the first of many grinding grammatical gear shifts I'd have to make in life as a military wife and, most importantly, as a Christian under command of the King to communicate His truth to others.

As a result, the origin and development of words has always fascinated me. The study of a word's ancestry is known as etymology (not to be confused with entomology…study of bugs!). The etymology of American English, how our nation's version of the Queen's

English came about, is a subject I enjoy. America's earliest settlers brought with them not only their hopes and dreams, but their languages, expressions, and slang as well. The Irish, Germans, and Scots settled my old stomping grounds of the south. The English and the Irish forged the northeast. Spaniards and American pioneers settled among the Native Americans in the southwest. The Spanish, French, and Caribbean nations populated Louisiana's coastline. Newcomers came in contact with natives and with others who spoke different languages and dialects. Gradually they blended and new forms of English were birthed. I could go down that rabbit trail for hours. My point is today we have one nation with many renditions of English.

Understanding one another "from sea to shining sea" is quite an undertaking in linguistic interpretation. What you impart and imply, I may not infer simply because our versions of English and our exposure differ so greatly. At times the experience is laughable. Other times the gaps can harm budding relationships, put a halt to business deals, and hinder the spread of the gospel.

Each of us has a colloquial collection, a set of words and phrases we use to communicate every day, a lexicon based on where we've lived, worked, and traveled. Likewise, each of us has an individual *faith language*, a powerful potpourri of speech originating in the people and experiences that taught us about God.

As we attempt to define truth to others, we must remember that even our fellow English speakers will decipher and decode our messages in their own language, that is, based on their own experiences, context, and culture.

Born and raised in America's Bible Belt, I could speak southern belle believer's lingo with amazing ease at the tender age of three. Although I had to forego the theology behind most of the terminology, I could readily rattle off the buzzwords of the faith as smoothly as any PK (preacher's kid). By age nine, I knew I was "redeemed by the blood of the Lamb"; however, it took several added years and maturity to understand that Christ was God's sacrifice on our behalf and that this "Lamb" wasn't the one who followed Mary to school in the nursery rhyme. My three-year-old daughter sings, "Be *exhausted*, O Lord, above the heavens." Later she will more fully comprehend what it means to *exalt* the Lord. Presently, she thinks of "Father Abraham" as her other daddy. She, like all believers, new and seasoned, will gradually adopt a style of ecclesiastical expression, a doctrinal dialect, that only those inside the body of Christ speak *and* understand.

Christians are familiar with the Great Commission: Jesus's command to "Go into all the world and preach the good news" (Mark 16:15) and to "go and make disciples of all nations, baptizing them in the name of the Father and of the Son and of the Holy Spirit, and teaching them to obey everything I have commanded you" (Matthew 28:19–20). Too often, however, we share our faith with unbelievers in a language foreign to them—Christianese. To them, a *conversion* is still a money exchange term. They don't *redeem* anything but coupons. To them, to *justify* means to get even. A *conviction* is still a prison sentence, *grace* is something they recite at the dinner table, and, being *righteous* means being totally cool.

Nick at Night

Most Christian jargon is as difficult for unbelievers to comprehend today as the phrase "born again" sounded to Nicodemus 2,000 years ago. **Read John 3:1–12.**

What do you learn about Nicodemus from verse 1?

_____

_____

The Pharisees were members of a Jewish group of about 6,000 men that began around 150 B.C. They lived in every city and village in Israel (Luke 5:17). They emphasized the strict interpretation and observance of the Law given to Israel through Moses. Many Pharisees were not truly godly men, but were hypocritical, proud, and lovers of position and power among the Jewish people; however, some were sincere in their devotion to and pursuit of God. I think Nicodemus was one of these few.

What did Nicodemus know about Jesus (v. 2)?

_____

_____

What first attracted Nicodemus to Jesus (v. 2)?

_____

_____

Where was Jesus doing these miracles? Read John 2:23.

_____

Why was Jesus in that particular city?

_____

_____

The majority of Pharisees despised Jesus and rejected His claim of sonship to God. Getting back to John 3, with what was Nicodemus struggling (v. 2)?

_____

_____

_____

_____

What was Jesus's reply to Nicodemus? Write out verse 3 here:

_____

_____

_____

Concealed by the collage of black and gray shadows of night, perhaps under the breeze-kissed branches of a sprawling olive tree, Jesus addressed Nicodemus's desire to see the kingdom of God's light. Jesus knew that Nicodemus needed much more than a teacher. He knew that Nick needed a Savior.

Instructors and instruction are a dime a dozen. Do you know someone who has an abundance of head knowledge but has an empty heart that aches for the truth? Write that person's name here.

_____

What instruction threw Nick for a loop? What did he ask?

_____

_____

_____

Remember, a Pharisee interpreted God's Word _strictly_. The emphasis of a Pharisee's life was _self_-righteousness, his bedrock belief being that God's blessings are only for those who perfectly keep the Law.

Based on your knowledge of the person you named as having abundant head knowledge but an empty heart, describe how he or she views the Bible?

_____

_____

What is the emphasis of that person's life?

_____

_____

What is his or her core belief regarding the meaning of life?

_____

_____

What experiences do you think have influenced that person's beliefs?

_____

_____

Jesus knew what the Pharisees thought (Luke 5:22). He also knew exactly how they reasoned, how their logic went, how they interpreted the Word, the language of God. **Reread Nick's flabbergasted response in John 3:4.** Do you hear his frustration? Do you hear his cry beneath that frustration? Jesus did, too. Jesus was not derailed by Nick's determination to fit God's wisdom into man's matrix for the meaning of life.

What roadblocks have you run up against as you've shared your faith with the person you named above?

_____

_____

_____

_____

_____

_____

How did you respond to that roadblock?

_____

_____

_____

Read John 3:5–9. How did Jesus respond to Nick's roadblock (vv. 5–8)?

_____

_____

_____

Was that the end of Nick's confusion (v. 9)?

_____

Jesus always comforts the one who cries for truth, even when those cries are camouflaged by headstrongness, humanity, or a broken heart. Jesus handled Nick's hurdle, the necessity of being "born again," with a perfect blend of authority, composure, and compassion, a mix that comes only from heaven's heart. Jesus didn't give up on Nicodemus. In His signature style, Christ answered the questioner with a question (John 3:10, 12). He knows what works with whom.

Jesus knew everything Nicodemus was thinking. He heard Nick's unspoken thoughts loud and clear. He hears the heart of your loved one, too. He can enable you to learn the language of your loved one's heart. He can enable you to respectfully go over, under, or around every roadblock with supernatural grace, wisdom, and courage. By His Spirit that lives inside of you, He will bring to your mind and mouth just the right words, the perfect illustration, and the clear explanation for which your loved one silently cries.

DAY 3

*O*ften, Jesus taught the people about God, His purposes and plans, and kingdom issues in parables: short, simple, easy-to-remember, stories that embodied divine truth, an applicable lesson, or an apt answer. This wasn't a style He picked up at toastmaster meetings. No, His teaching tactics were intentional. Those familiar with the prophets' ancient writings should have recognized Jesus's presentation style as a telltale sign that He was Israel's expected Messiah.

Read Matthew 13:10–17. Although uneducated, Jesus's disciples picked up on His pattern. They wanted to know why the Prince of heaven preferred parables. What had been given to the disciples (v. 11)?

_____

_____

To whom had this *not* been given?

_____

_____

Jesus said, "Whoever has will be given more, and he will have an abundance. Whoever does not have, even what he has will be taken from him" (Matthew 13:12). **How did Jesus describe the people of Israel (vv. 13–15)?**

_____

_____

_____

Jesus did not lump His disciples together with the spiritually dull. What is the condition of the *believer's* eyes and ears (vv. 16–17)?

_____

_____

_____

_____

The people following and listening to Jesus were a challenging mix of the spiritually dull and the spiritually dead. That could be said about many churches today. Not much has changed in 2,000 years!

God, in His measureless patience and mercy, communicated through His Son great pillars of truth to the spiritually dull and dead using parables, short stories with believable characters in settings that were familiar to the ordinary person. Simply, He communicated within His listeners' context. He lovingly, purposefully, and patiently spoke the language of His listeners.

Turnkey Truth

We, like Nicodemus, must understand that before we will be able to perceive the truths tucked throughout Jesus's teachings, we must be born again. We must be given newness of spirit and mind in order for our souls to savor the Savior's words. This is the key to having "the knowledge of the secrets of the kingdom." Without new birth, hearts remain calloused; eyes and ears remain closed.

Truth eludes those who are not born again. A corpse sees and hears nothing. What is the message of salvation to the one who is not born again? Read 1 Corinthians 1:18.

_____

_____

What is that same message to the one who is born again?

_____

_____

What is the difference between the two? New eyes. New ears. New heart. New understanding. New ability to unearth the truth treasures God has tucked throughout His eternal Word. No matter how many ways we try to translate the truth of God to our loved one, it falls on deaf ears until he or she first believes and is born again. And that, my friend, is solely the work of the Holy Spirit. We can't birth baby believers. Only God can do this by His Spirit. Our responsibility is to love others in the language they recognize and understand, to choose our words prayerfully, and then to leave the translation of it all to God.

Jesus recognized that the people spoke a different language. Because their hearts were calloused and darkened, they could no longer see, recognize, or understand God's truth; therefore, He spoke their native tongue—not only a Galilean dialect of Aramaic, but the language of their hearts. To the baker, He expressed Himself as the Bread of life. To those tending their flocks, He showed Himself to be the Good Shepherd and the Lamb of God. To the disillusioned wives, He said He was the perfect Bridegroom. To the tax collector, He spoke of Himself as hidden treasure. To the weary, thirsty, and used-up woman at the well, He offered living water. To the candle maker, He was the Light of the world. To the physician, He was the Cure. To the lawyer, He was the True Advocate. To the mistreated widow, He was the righteous Judge. To the soldier, he was the Mighty Warrior. To the carpenter, he was the Door. To the gardener, He was the True Vine. To the writer, he was the Author of faith and salvation. To the minister, He was the High Priest. To the deceived, He was the Spirit of

Truth. To the architectural engineer, He was the Cornerstone. To the lost and wandering, He was the Way. To the imprisoned, He was the Deliverer. To a new kingdom, He was the King.

So neither he who plants nor he who waters is anything,
but only God, who makes things grow.
—1 Corinthians 3:7

DAY 4

*t*hink about the challenges you personally face today as a woman, as a wife, as a mother. **Describe in a few simple phrases your current challenges in each area.**

As a wife

_____

_____

As a mother

_____

_____

As a homemaker

_____

_____

As a member of your extended family

_____

_____

As an employee/businesswoman/co-worker

_____

_____

As a neighbor

_____

_____

Whether you are aware of it or not, you are presently enrolled in a lifelong communications course. The situations and people you listed above are your instructors. You are a student of linguistics, learning a language you will need later in life to be God's messenger to a particular person or group of people. God is using your current circumstances, the welcome blessings as well as the tough trials, to train your tongue to speak a language that will translate life to the spirit of a certain someone in your future.

I believe that in God's economy, heartaches and sorrows are never wasted. Let me use my life as an example. For more than 20 years, I have loved, served, and followed my military husband around the world. Looking back, I see now that the loneliness, fear, tests, single parenting, separations, moves, and general madness were actually my instructors incognito on assignment from God! He was teaching me a language spoken by women around the world, the language of the heart of the military wife. God had _you_ in mind as he held _my_ feet to the fire all those years. The daily struggles that seemed insurmountable menaces were, in reality, effective masked mentors carefully chosen and sent by God into my life. His mission has been to accomplish something larger than me, through me, to reach a people group only He could have imagined my life would influence. He is continually doing the same in the lives of each of His children, including you!

After the first step, being born again, I took a second step: listening to the Lord as He painstakingly taught me—through the happy moments and through the heartaches—the vocabulary and unique vernacular of a very specific group of women, the wives of military servicemen worldwide. None of it was textbook knowledge. Believe me, it's been 100% hands-on training. Now I can look back and actually praise God for the pain! The difficulties that chased me into my Father's arms have begun to bear fruit, a harvest of hope for those on a similar exhausting uphill climb.

Look again at the descriptions of your present life's challenges that you listed previously. Identify the one you are wrestling with most intensely today, and write it here.

_____

_____

Read 2 Corinthians 1:3–7. In the NIV, Paul gives us three descriptions of God in verse 3. What are they?

God is the Father of our _____

God is the Father of _____

God is the God of all _____

In verse 4, Paul tells us that there is an underlying reason why God comforts us in our troubles. What is that reason?

_____

_____

_____

_____

The Holy Spirit, writing to us through Paul, makes it clear that pain is not pointless. Why are troubles and stress a part of God's design for our lives (v. 6)?

Yes, God is committed to conforming us to the likeness of His Son (Romans 8:29). He desires that we grow strong in Christ to full maturity; however, God's greater goal goes beyond us. His aim is to reach the many others who suffer similarly. He is preparing us to bring to them the comfort of God they desperately crave.

Let me ask you a question. Are you listening to your "teachers"? Are you applying His Word to your circumstances and learning from them what God wants to reveal about Himself to you?

God has promised to never leave you. He has promised to comfort you in all the trials He designs and allows and to refine you through them. Not only this, but He will, in His time, comfort many countless others through you as you trust Him and stay open to His leading. He is equipping you to speak to them in word and deed in the unique language of compassion that the trials have taught you along the way.

★ DAY 5

 marvel at the beauty of God's ways. I have wondered why God sent a red, wrinkled newborn to struggling, poverty-stricken newlyweds. I have contemplated God's perfect reasoning in anointing a low-class, uneducated carpenter to engrave Jehovah's name in the heart of a splintered world.

How old was Jesus when He began His public ministry? Read Luke 3:23.

I have puzzled over why Jesus waited until He was 30 years old to begin His public work. I believe God wanted to learn my language. He emptied Himself of all His riches and rights to walk miles and miles in my moccasins. Jesus was immersed in our world for a third of a century, experiencing all and more than I ever will. Through His temptation, rejection, poverty, tears, laughter, hard work, family struggles, tested friendships, consistent faith, and commitment to obeying His Father against all odds, Jesus learned my language!

What did Jesus call Himself in John 10:14?

Jesus is our ultimate example as we, His undershepherds, reach out to others with the gospel. There is a flock out there in need of your shepherding skills. There is a flock, a group of people with whom you deeply connect, wandering about, scared and vulnerable. God is uniquely shaping and outfitting you to speak His truth, His comfort to them in the language they understand.

Jesus's 30 years of listening should be my model. Too often, I listen briefly to a friend's words of woe, then blurt out a pat cliché—"Trust God; I'll be praying for you" or "Just keep the faith." In reality, my language is foreign to my friend and my words are salt on her open wounds. If I would follow Jesus's example and listen long before I speak, perhaps I would learn the language of my friend's heart. I then would be better equipped to express comfort and truth in words she fully understands; however, learning the language of a friend's heart is costly. It requires patience, effort, and lots of precious, priceless time, but that is true for any linguistic endeavor.

Read Philippians 2:5–8. What was the price Jesus paid to translate the heart of the Father to us in the way we needed and could understand?

_____

_____

_____

_____

Learning the language of the human heart cost Jesus His glory, His life, His all, and He did it solely to restore God-to-man/man-to-God communication. We too must discipline ourselves to listen to others, learn their language, then choose our words carefully. So much power and accuracy can be contained in one small word. One chosen word can entirely change the course of a friend's life. Before time began, Jesus's name was "the Word." This one chosen Word perfectly expressed God's character, completely fulfilled His purpose, and totally changed the course of history.

An Invitation from Jesus

Dear One,

I know you intimately. I love you deeply. I am intensely interested in the details of your life. I am completely aware of the special physical, emotional, and spiritual needs you have as the wife of a serviceman. I, too, am a warrior. The Lord is My name. I, your loving Savior, want to be actively involved in your life.

I leave the first step up to you. Everything in My creation has a first, a beginning. Everybody has a birthday. Every book begins with a first page. Every song begins with a first note. Every journey begins with the first step. Likewise, your search for personal wholeness has a proper beginning.

The first step toward true contentment is entrance into a right relationship with God, through Me, Jesus Christ, His Son. I am the Alpha and the Omega, the Beginning and the End. Believing in Me is the beginning of a right relationship with God. I, God the Son, who existed before time as part of the Holy Trinity, humbled Myself more than 2,000 years ago, became flesh, and lived among you.

God's standard of perfection was not within anyone's reach because of sin. Everyone missed the mark, except Me. I lived a perfect life, a life without sin, unlike the rest of men and women. My Father loved *you* so much that He gave Me, His only begotten Son, that whoever believes in Me should not die, but have everlasting life. By dying on the cross, I paid your debt to God that you could never pay. My Father has promised that you can know and enjoy the fullness of His love and His exciting plan for your life if you believe and trust in Me as your one and only Hope. If you choose not to believe, you will one day die and be separated from God forever.

Eternal life is a free gift from My Father for you. Just say with your mouth that I am Lord of your life and believe in your heart that God raised Me from the dead; then you will be saved. I will forgive your sin and remove all your shame, once and for all.

I promise to then give you a new heart and put a new spirit in you. I will remove from you your heart of stone and give you a heart of flesh. I will put My Spirit in you to move you to follow My decrees and be careful to keep My laws.

I am at the door of your heart, knocking. If you hear My voice and open the door, I will come in to you and eat with you, and you with Me. We will have unbreakable togetherness forever.

Love,
Jesus Christ

Exodus 15:3; Revelation 1:8; Revelation 22:13; John 3:16; Acts 2:38–39; Romans 3:23; Romans 6:23; Romans 10:9–10; Hebrews 9:26–28; Ezekiel 36:26–27; Revelation 3:20

Hope for the Home Front Bible Study

Ministry Contact Information

For more information about resources and events
or to schedule speaking engagements, visit
http://www.hopeforthehomefront.com
or contact us by phone.

One Hope Ministry
Phone: 1-757-681-HOPE (1-757-681-4673)
Monday–Friday
9:00 A.M.–5:00 P.M. EST

Personal Letters and Email Welcomed
One Hope Ministry
P. O. Box 1165
Monument, Colorado 80132-1165
USA
marshele.waddell@onehopeministry.com

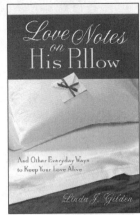
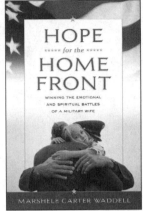
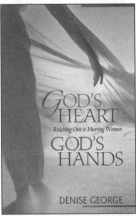
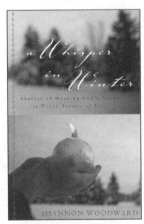

New Hope® Publishers is a division of WMU®,
an international organization that challenges Christian believers
to understand and be radically involved in God's mission.
For more information about WMU, go to www.wmu.com.
More information about New Hope books may be found at
www.newhopepublishers.com. New Hope books
may be purchased at your local bookstore.